THE PRINCETON SERIES IN
NINETEENTH-CENTURY ART,
CULTURE, AND SOCIETY

In the Theater of
Criminal Justice

IN THE THEATER
OF CRIMINAL JUSTICE

The Palais de Justice in Second Empire Paris

by Katherine Fischer Taylor

PRINCETON UNIVERSITY PRESS

PRINCETON · NEW JERSEY

Copyright © 1993 by Princeton University Press
Published by Princeton University Press, 41 William Street,
Princeton, New Jersey 08540
In the United Kingdom: Princeton University Press, Chichester, West Sussex

Library of Congress Cataloging-in-Publication Data
Taylor, Katherine Fischer.
In the theater of criminal justice : the Palais de justice in Second
Empire Paris / Katherine Fischer Taylor.
p.   cm. — (Princeton series in nineteenth-century art,
culture, and society)
Includes bibliographical references and index.
ISBN 0-691-03214-9
1. Palais de justice (Paris, France)   2. Signs and symbols in
architecture.   3. Allegories.   4. Architecture and society—France—
History—19th century.   5. Justice and politics—France—History—19th
century.   6. Paris (France)—Buildings, structures,
etc. I. Title. II. Series.
NA4475.F82P378   1993
725′.15′0944361—dc20   92-34680

This book has been composed in Galliard

Princeton University Press books are printed on acid-free paper and meet the
guidelines for permanence and durability of the Committee on Production
Guidelines for Book Longevity of the Council on Library Resources

Printed in the United States of America

Designed by Laury A. Egan

10 9 8 7 6 5 4 3 2 1

10 9 8 7 6 5 4 3 2 1
(Pbk.)

CONTENTS

For Woodman

LIST OF ILLUSTRATIONS

ACKNOWLEDGMENTS

M Y FIRST acknowledgment is to the *monde* of the Palais de Justice of Paris, which welcomed me in the 1980s as a graduate student studying the modernization of that historic building, and continues to accommodate my curiosity as it has expanded further into social history. Those who have helped are too numerous and various to name here, but I would like to single out the Secretariat of the Court of Appeals, currently headed by Alain Girardet. The types of questions asked in this book owe a great deal to my colleagues at the University of Chicago. For the time to ponder them, I am most grateful to the J. Paul Getty Foundation for a 1990–1991 postdoctoral fellowship and to the University for granting me a leave. I have benefited from two presentations related to this essay, the first, at David Van Zanten's invitation, in a symposium at Northwestern University on the monumental form of Paris, and the second at the University of Chicago's Workshop on Interdisciplinary Approaches to Modern France, organized by Colin Lucas and Jan Goldstein. Among the many who commented on this work in draft, I would like to thank especially Jan Goldstein, Neil Levine, Sarah Maza, Linda Seidel, Joel Snyder—and Woodman Taylor, for his sustained interest in a project that never seemed to try his patience.

INTRODUCTION

FRENCH JUSTICE was rarely talked about in the 19th century without reference to the dramatic change from ancien régime to modern justice, a change identified with the historic Palais de Justice of Paris, where French centralized justice had been founded centuries earlier. This transformation was informed by the larger cultural revolution of the Enlightenment, which latter 20th-century theorists and historians have described as the replacement of icons by texts, a substitution that would seem to explain the difference between two images of the chief courtroom at the Palais before and after the Revolution (figs. 1, 2).[1] A view of the room in 1787, showing its rich decoration and sculpted ceiling, displays the icon, the king on his *lit de justice* in the

1. Grand'Chambre, or chief courtroom of the Parlement of Paris, during the *lit de justice* of Louis XVI on November 19, 1787, engraving by C. Niquet after a drawing by Meunier and Girardet.

FOUQUIER - THINVILLE JUGÉ PAR LE TRIBUNAL RÉVOLUTIONNAIRE ,
le 12 Floréal An 3me de la République

2. Grand'Chambre during the trial of Fouquier-Tinville by the temporarily installed Revolutionary Tribunal, 12 floréal an III (1795).

corner, from whom all authority flows in pyramidal form to the nation, represented by the judicial body of Parlement. The prestigious room was appropriated, reoriented and stripped for duty by the new Supreme Court, which considered the early French Renaissance decor inappropriate for a courtroom ruled by an ideal of codified law. This essay is about what happened to the representation of French justice in the Second Empire, specifically in the new wing for the criminal courts, or Cour d'assises, opened in 1868 to much critical debate (fig. 56). Why readopt rich decoration, which was explicitly associated with the vanished French Renaissance decor of the chief courtroom? What did it imply about justice and authority, and their operation, in the volatile political climate of the 19th century?

In fact, the schema that text replaces icon does not fit the modernization of

French justice during the Revolution and the Napoleonic Empire when one turns from law, and its basis in king or code, to courtroom procedure. Notwithstanding the indisputable importance of written law, the codes were mediated by procedure. And if written codes replaced the live king as the ultimate source of justice, procedure made a reverse transformation. Especially in the criminal courts, the change was from written, secret proceedings to emphasis on publicity and oral proceedings, and hence live spectacle (figs. 3, 4). The issue of authority is central here. The late 18th century's allegory of Justice, reliant on her book, represented a system that depended on experts to make decisions; 19th-century Justice, based on orality, instead weighs the evidence she hears and casts her ballot in an urn, representing the lay jury, which France had adopted only during the Revolution and had maintained solely for the criminal courts. In short, modern French justice instituted two kinds of publicity, one doctrinal—the

3. Allegory of Law, by Gois, 1780s, staircase from the main east vestibule (galerie Mercière) to the Cour d'appel, Paris.

4. Allegory of Justice, by Jaley, 1868, bas-relief in the west facade of the Palais de Justice, Paris.

text of the codes, available to a reading public—and one procedural—the oral trial open to the public. If these modes were meant to reinforce one another, they separated in practice over the course of the 19th century, particularly in the criminal courts. And certainly they carried different implications for construing architecture as the framework for practice: the building as a neutral setting for the work of internal meditation prompted by texts, or as a theater for social activity in which architecture interacts with the institution to shape its meaning.

The sculptures belong to different sections of the historic Palais, actually to two opposing entrance facades (figs. 5,6). Facing east is a neoclassical entrance courtyard built to replace medieval buildings in the 18th century, just before the Revolution; here textual Justice presides. Facing west is a vast addition inaugurated in the Second Empire, whose facade includes Justice with her urn and leads directly to the new criminal courtroom. As the most monumental part of a comprehensive 19th-century

5. East facade of the Palais, showing the entrance courtyard (cour du Mai) by Desmaisons and Moreau-Desproux, 1781ff., flanked by the early 17th-century waiting hall to the right (Salle des pas perdus) and the 13th-century Sainte-Chapelle to the left. Lithograph by Benoist, c. 1861.

6. West facade of the Palais, Duc, Dommey and Daumet. Photograph by Marville, between June 1875, when the new staircase and entrance opened to the public, and the photographer's death in 1878.

renovation of the Palais, the architecture of the Second Empire wing was viewed by critics as a representation of modern, revised justice.

The Second Empire's criminal courts presented a controversial departure from the persistent representation of justice as textual and abstract. For the first half of the 19th century, Justice's book became the Napoleonic codes, texts that were held to be so clear, simple and universally applicable that they minimized the significance and procedure of the trial itself; the law was self-evident and absolute, and judge and juror merely applied it. That representation ignored notorious problems of procedure, particularly the peculiar hybrid of written and oral proceedings established by Napoléon for the criminal courts. In procedural terms, textual justice traditionally meant secret, professional judgment, while the principle of publicity established by the Revolution was predicated on orality. To represent justice in the new criminal courts as live, ceremonial spectacle was to broach these problems, and in so doing, to take on the more general challenge of reviving iconicity when its traditional subject, the ruler, had been displaced by a diffuse new subject, the public.

metropolis

In architectural and urbanistic terms, the Palais remains one of the central monuments of Paris, riding one end of the île de la Cité at the core of the city (fig. 15). With its 19th-century facade overlooking the prow-like place Dauphine towards the palace of the Louvre downstream, and its 18th-century courtyard fronting the revitalized north-south artery of the city, it commanded a strategic position in the symbolic and practical topography of Paris as recreated in the 19th century. The building itself demands attention as a physical object, as does its place in the remade city. But monumentality is nothing without audience. The 19th-century map of Paris has long been said to concern circulation; it is essential to take stock of the flow of people among its monuments, a diversity of crowds that experienced those buildings as social institutions and artifacts.

This essay explores the social institution that the architecture of the Palais was supposed to represent: first, the system of criminal justice, which was one of the most popular spectacles of Paris, precisely because of its uneasy mix of the oral and the written, and secondly, the way architecture participated in that spectacle and crystallized debates about justice as a reflection of society. It focuses on conflicts over the locus of the authority to judge in post-Revolutionary France, on problems of legibility and meaning in interpreting physical evidence in court and in interpreting architecture, and on the way these debates were couched in visualizable but ambiguous terms such as gender and class which were extended both to trials and to the courthouse itself, and which help to clarify the interrelationship of architecture and its public. It looks at these issues through 19th-century commentary on two events: the first major trial in the new courtroom, and the unusual inauguration of the criminal courts wing in 1868. After an extended analysis of the theatrical aspects of the trial—rules and dynamics, setting, choreography, audience and cast, plot and thematics—it moves to a brief historical commentary situating that trial within the dynamic history of views on the right to punish during the 19th century. It concludes with a coda on the critical controversy over the architecture stirred by the inauguration. Congruent with the subject of judgment, its method entails calculated insistence upon detail.[2]

The Trial

THE TRIAL of Jean-Baptiste Troppmann was the first to draw the public en masse to the new criminal courts. Held from December 28 to 30, 1869, it took place a year after the court's inauguration amid the agitation of the late liberal phase of the Empire. The public, from emperor to populace, had followed the case in the press for three months, from the discovery of the crime through Troppmann's arrest and the investigation. What they knew was that Troppmann was a poor Alsatian mechanic, barely 20, charged with the single-handed murder of an entire family, whose bodies were publicly displayed for identification in the Morgue near the Palais (fig. 7).[3] The motive was thought to be a misfired attempt to abscond with the life savings of the successful working class parents. Troppmann first poisoned the father, Jean Kinck, whom he had lured into an Alsatian forest with promises that he could invest in a counterfeit-money enterprise concealed in a ruin. When Troppmann failed to lay hands on Kinck's capital, he lured the rest of the family to a rendezvous at the Gare du

Achille Kinck et la petite Marie.   Alfred Kinck.   Henri Kinck.   Emile Kinck.   Madame Kinck.

Les six premiers cadavres exposés à la Morgue.

7. Cadavers of Troppmann's victims, as displayed through the public vitrine at the Paris Morgue.

Nord in Paris, hoping they would bring the family savings. Taking mother and children to a field in the quasi-industrial hinterland northeast of Paris, he strangled, stabbed, and buried them. He then fled to Le Havre, to sail for America, but was arrested for his suspicious appearance. The detective police rapidly identified him with the bodies and the press swelled with the investigation. Indeed, the public helped dig up the bodies, and the field at Pantin became a site for pilgrimage and picnic (fig. 8). The penalty for premeditated murder was death, and the press correctly predicted—indeed advocated—that outcome (fig. 27). The public had already had its spectacles, even glimpses of Troppmann. What drew it from the field to the courthouse, when the drama of the trial and its outcome seemed resolved?[4]

A recent jurist has suggested that a trial is two dramas, that of the case nested within that of the courtroom proceedings.[5] Knowing the case, the public seems to have come for the proceedings. At the simplest level of event, it could have gathered from the press that the proceedings would revolve around Troppmann's late assertion that he had accomplices, and the prosecution's unwillingness to pursue his fragmentary clues. The court did not change this decision, suggesting that the haste to prosecute Troppmann without exhaustive investigation had to do with the government's need for a surrogate for public anger over the regime's own performance. If this is so, content merged with proceedings, for the case was argued in terms of misplaced individual ambition and its challenge to patriarchal authority—themes that echoed tensions in the judicial system pitting the jury against the prosecution and bench.

LE CRIME DE PANTIN. — Fouilles à la charrue ordonnées par l'autorité dans la journée du 27 septembre sur le terrain du crime.

8. Search for the bodies of Troppmann's victims, field at Pantin, 1869.

The Judicial System

IT IS WORTH remembering that 19th-century French expectations of the trial were culturally and historically specific. Americans are fond of declaring that in France a defendant is guilty until proven innocent. That erroneous dictum does express an essential cultural difference: the French grant a more authoritative and active role to the prosecution and judges in both the investigation and the trial. To make sense of this and, ultimately, its representation, we need to look first at French justice as a system.

An explanation is in order for why existing accounts of French justice need to be reframed here. The criminal trial demonstrates a difficult relationship between law and procedure which obtains both in 19th-century judicial practice and, historiographically, in accounts of modern French justice. In France, jurists write the history of justice and frame its doctrine; in histories, they have traditionally favored doctrine over practice. While procedure has its doctrine—there are codes of procedure to complement the codes of civil and penal law—procedure also has a social history of implementation, which is only beginning to be studied. Yet jurists most commonly emphasize the *longue durée* of post-Revolutionary doctrine, expressing a preference for principle over practice, but perhaps also tactfully underplaying some ways in which penal procedure has tended to undermine and revise doctrine.[6]

There are two major exceptions to this pattern. The first is the historical commentary of certain turn-of-the-century jurists who were attempting to justify the changes they advocated in Third Republic criminal justice; we will return to this in the second part of this essay. The other is a current initiative dating to the 1980s, stimulated in some measure by Michel Foucault's critique of the humanitarian discourse of the Enlightenment, which was itself critical to the reformulation of modern French justice and to its practice in the 19th century. Foucault established new terms for the discussion of authority in post-Revolutionary France, arguing that the juridical rights exemplified in court had been infiltrated and overridden by a network of disciplinary practices and techniques which we, as their subjects, need to recognize. Yet Foucault himself refused to look at the dynamics of the courtroom. Even while pointing out the transference of public judicial spectacle from extravagant corporal punishment in the ancien régime to the assessment of psychological guilt and responsibility in the post-Revolutionary trial, Foucault insisted on the need to look away from the central spectacle to the margins—in the case of the penal system, to the prison. In so doing, he pointed out that the courtroom trial entailed a mixture of modes of power, both the juridical system predicated on sovereign rights and the disciplinary techniques based on normalization and individuation which he himself mapped in other contexts. Characterizing these modes in visual terms, Foucault related sovereignty to spectacle or display, and discipline to an all-surveying gaze, and discounted spectacle as an appropriate object for study.[7]

As historians have taken up the challenge of modern French justice as a dynamic discursive practice many have begun with the disciplinary roles of the French magistrate or the psychiatric presence in the trial, and with the status of the defendant as social deviant.[8] In seeking to understand judicial practice as the more complex interplay that Foucault acknowledged, however, I have chosen not to take up Foucault's terms directly. Rather than attempt to identify the disciplinary as opposed to the sovereign aspects of the trial (and in order to avoid the mistake of equating procedure with discipline, as against sovereign doctrine), I am framing the problem in terms of the dynamics of written and oral procedures, terms that will permit me to handle in a way somewhat different from Foucault, the role of looking and of visual display in the trial, and, I hope, in Second Empire culture. For I am concerned not only to highlight the dynamic aspects of the trial, but also to draw attention to its spectacular performative character, which is essential to its architecture.[9]

We have already identified one feature that distinguished the code of law from procedure: that the code exemplified the principle of textual publicity, appealing to a reading public, while procedure depended on oral publicity, exemplified by the criminal jury. Here we can elaborate: procedure emphasized orality, but it also distinguished the jury's judgment on the basis of oral evidence from a knowledge and implementation of law, which was the province solely of the presiding judges. In this distinction, French criminal justice resembled British practice. But in France, the professional judge also directed oral proceedings, based on his access to written documents concerning the case assembled before the trial. The French explanation of this arrangement has been couched in terms of a historical definition of juridical models.

Jurists have described the French system and its history in terms of an inquisitorial model versus an accusatorial one.[10] The inquisitorial model formerly implemented by the courtroom judge survived in the modern offices of the public prosecutor or state's attorney (which France invented and bequeathed to other nations) and of the French examining magistrate or *juge d'instruction* (such as Simenon, the 20th-century writer of *romans policiers*, has familiarized), who interrogates penal suspects in the privacy of his office before the case goes to trial (fig. 9). In schematic terms, this model gives primacy to the judge, who personally questions suspects and litigants, directs investigation of the evidence, and judges the case; it is associated with written law, evidence, and expertise, and it exemplifies deductive reasoning. In physical terms, it implies a hierarchical axis of power flowing from the knowing judge to his subject. By contrast, the accusatorial model entails an oral duel in public between the accuser and the accused, such as the artist Honoré Daumier parodied in his watercolor, "Une cause célèbre" (fig. 10).[11] The contest is fought across a symmetrically divided court-

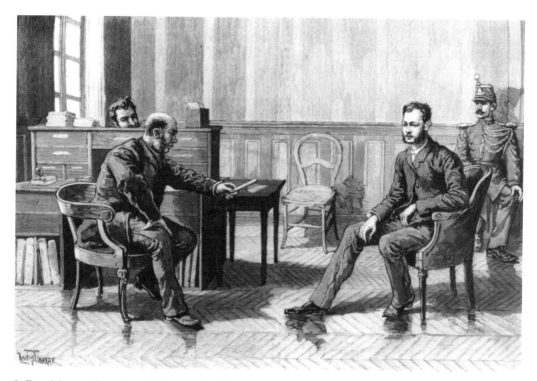

9. Examining magistrate Guillot interrogating the suspect Pranzini in his office at the Paris Palais, 1887.

10. Honoré Daumier, "Une cause célèbre," pen, crayon and watercolor, undated [c. 1858/1862].

room before a passive judge, who decides the case inductively on the basis of the proceedings he witnesses. Historically this model is associated with common law and oral procedure in the Middle Ages and particularly with Anglo-Saxon practice and its empirical bias. The inquisitorial model was adopted in France under absolutism as a philosophy of judicial authority exercised most energetically in penal cases. Though the Napoleonic codes tempered it with greater rights for the defendant, it has never been fully renounced.

The Napoleonic legal system established lasting compromises between these two models—different compromises in each jurisdiction, giving each a different character. Most important is the systematic distinction between penal and civil justice. Civil justice set the standard for the judicial system as a whole, because it addressed points of law, reasoned with erudition, and was decided by professional judges. Penal justice was considered exceptional and far less prestigious, for it revolved around points of fact and moral credibility, which are accessible to laymen and thus may be judged by a jury.[12] From the professional viewpoint, a lay court was an unpredictable, inelegant affair which required compensatory management. Hence a difference in procedure.[13] Civil trials, which revolve around expertise, paradoxically entail accusatorial counter-arguments in front of a passive judge. Criminal trials employ oral testimony and argument in court before a lay jury, but chasten it with inquisitorial control by the presiding judge and special privileges for the prosecution. Indeed, the persistent inquisitorial rationale of penal justice is plain in the misdemeanors courts, where there is no jury, and, if the judge so decides, no witness testimony.[14] The exceptional use of abundant oral testimony and a jury in the criminal courts gave visible guarantees to defendants faced with only the severest penalties.

This situation led such eminent French jurists as Esmein and Garraud to characterize criminal justice as "eclectic," a "compromise" between models. Such a compromise did not lack purpose. From a professional magistrate's point of view, the criminal jury was but the representative of an actual, potentially unruly public which the trial served to bring into alignment with that primary emblem of sovereign will, the timeless Napoleonic codes. In other words, modern sovereignty was lodged in the codes, and trials functioned as the vehicle for realizing it, and perhaps also for teaching the public how to apply that general set of principles which constituted the codes in contingent daily life. Magistrates required authoritative (inquisitorial) powers to effect that fusion of live and textual publicity in the courtroom. And yet the very compromise meant to effect fusion was labelled a source of "strife . . . between . . . two tendencies" by Esmein (although he observed that the accusatorial aspects offered enough of a semblance of protection for the defense that they served politically to blunt public criticism of the inquisitorial aspects of the trial and stymie a perpetual reform movement). As for the jury and the public, they were notorious for not cooperating with the magistrature—for insisting on their own sovereignty, even for

8

contravening the code. And as the Napoleonic codes aged and the locus of sovereignty was redisputed in revolutions and sequential regimes, even the occasional magistrate declared that juries might serve to update the codes, bringing them into phase with changing social values. In short, the hybrid of models generated a history of tension between the magistrature and the jury. It was precisely the hybrid and anomalous character of the criminal court that reduced its prestige for the magistrature and guaranteed the fascination of the public.[15]

The 19th-century criminal trial in a sense recapitulated in its procedure its own historical evolution. In the inquisitorial criminal trial of the ancien régime, the judge questioned the accused in a closed chamber without informing him of the charges or evidence, and decided the case on the basis of his own investigation. Governing the verdict, however, were strict rules of legal proof which some jurists held to be as just as the witness testimony that replaced them in the modern trial. In 19th-century justice, the old procedure survived in the pretrial investigation. At the request of the public prosecutor, an examining magistrate questioned the suspect in private without a lawyer, assembled a dossier of evidence and witness depositions, and decided whether to propose the case for trial, where the prosecutor would take over (fig. 9). What occurred in the courtroom then was a sudden release of the defendant into a relatively balanced contest with the public prosecutor. This is what the trial offered to a public gorged on details leaked from the investigation.

The blending of the written investigation into the oral trial has experiential implications so important for the form and layout of the courtroom that they merit systematic discussion; taken for granted by those present at Troppmann's trial, they will serve here to help carry the reader into that event and its setting. Walter Ong's observations on the phenomenological differences between oral and literate cultures, while ahistorically framed, are suggestive for the different ritual dynamics of the two types of procedure.[16] A trial based on the reading of documents, presented and judged by experts, tends to abstract from and reflect on experience, distancing the listeners from the acts in question, their social context, and the sources of the evidence. Such reports also tend to be non-combative in tone, fostering a sense of impartial distance that amplifies their authority. The extreme case is the French Supreme Court or Cour de cassation, which dispassionately reconsiders cases solely in terms of whether due process has been respected; note the meditative postures of the justices as depicted in a popular magazine illustration of 1868 (fig. 11).[17] Oral testimony, because it re-presents events on the spot to an uninformed lay audience, tends to be agonistic and experiential; at its most effective, it revolves around facts and acts, described in narrative and gesture. It draws the listeners into a drama and unifies them in a common experience and values. Moreover, oral testimony blends evidence into performance, encouraging the listener to judge the credibility of the speaker as well as the statement. In French judicial philosophy, this constitutes a protection for the defen-

11. Grand'Chambre as the civil chamber of the Cour de cassation, Paris, Prosecutor Delangle giving his conclusions in the Lesurques case, 1868.

dant, but also a danger, for the most memorable witness or lawyer is the one who understands the rules of the oral performance and enters into the antagonistic speech, type characters, and other melodramatic devices that Ong and Peter Brooks have analyzed—without necessarily telling his or her truth.[18] It also encourages unexpected effects and dramatically timed introductions of unexpected evidence that French jurists disapprovingly term "incidents."[19]

The architectural effect of oral procedure is to convert the courtroom to a stage, in which space, sight lines and acoustics are critical. Anglo-Americans take that dramatic aspect for granted; but even ostensibly republican Frenchmen in the 19th century, because of their relatively recent adoption of public oral proceedings in criminal trials and the continued presence of inquisitorial features, experienced it as something persistently new and risky, and subject to checks.

The layout of the courtroom has much to tell about this situation, and was stable enough in the Second Empire to justify generalization (although we will later turn to aspects of the design of the Paris courtroom that challenged contemporary norms). The oral, agonistic courtroom is set up for viewing and hearing a seemingly balanced battle between prosecution and defense. The expert, inquisitorial courtroom is set up to enhance the authority of the judge or the system of justice he enforces; the furniture and decor define hierarchy and status which is reinforced by the ritual built into the proceedings. The French criminal courtroom of the mid-19th century looks symmetrical, for below the judges' bench lining the far end of the room, it is divided into equal halves equipped with similar boxes and benches (figs. 17, 54–56). The Anglo-American expects an accusatorial balance between prosecution and defense, such as obtained in the British criminal courtrooms at Old Bailey in London, where there was no public prosecutor until the late 19th century and where counsel for the accuser and the defendant both sat as equals in the center of the room (fig. 12).[20] The way the participants in the French trial occupy this setting, however, defies that construction of symmetry. The defendant and defense counsel take the dock and the bench below it at one side of the room. But it is the jury, rather than the prosecution, that faces the defense from the diametrically opposed box at the other side. While the prosecutor could be said to face the defense as well, it is from a skewed vantage point, for he occupies a chair at the far end of the judges' bench at the end of the room, indicating

12. Trial at the Central Criminal Courts (Old Bailey), London, based on drawing by Thomas Hosmer Shepherd, c. 1841–44.

11

his status as a magistrate. Victims or their representatives may sue for damages in a French criminal court, but when such a *partie civile* and counsel join a trial, they sit on the side of the defense, not the prosecution.

The social structure of the room has greater meaning when viewed in terms of state authority, for it is graded from the tribune for the magistrates (judges and prosecutors who are civil servants) at the far end of the long rectangle to the public at the opposite end. There are four zones, linked by the central aisle whose axis emanates from the presiding judge's chair. Below the zone defined by the magistrates' tribune is the *barreau*,[21] a large nearly empty enclosure centered on the bar where the witness stands and flanked by the jury and the defense counsel, who are both non-*fonction-naires* only temporarily invested with the professional authority necessary for the trial—a status irritatingly brought home to the lawyers at the beginning of each trial, when they were formally warned anew of their professional responsibilities to the court.[22] Beyond the gates of the *barreau* is a second enclosure, containing benches primarily destined for witnesses who represent a lesser degree of investment in the trial, sworn in only at the moment of their individual testimony to the court. Outside its gates stands the public, whose role is that of independent bystander with no formal responsibility toward the court except to obey the rules of order imposed by the presiding judge. The hierarchy of the inquisitorial courtroom is physically patent; it expresses and reinforces the inquisitorial aspect coloring French criminal trials in which the presiding judge actually conducts the questioning of the defendant and witnesses and directs the oral proceedings as a whole. The French proceedings were thus physically constructed as a contest between two visibly unequal entities: the individual defendant versus society, represented by the magistrates and, temporarily, by the jury. Nonetheless, we shall see that the proceedings offered the spectacle of a vigorous contest, not a unilateral imposition of social authority on the transgressing individual.

The relationship between physical structure and the character of the proceedings, as well as the tension between two different forms of procedure, was recognized by the French magistrate and politician Jean Cruppi in a protracted critique of the criminal courts at the end of the century. The historical context and purpose for Cruppi's reform proposal will be noted later, but for the moment his remarks can serve as a retrospective index of French self-consciousness about procedure and its architectural and ideological representation. Cruppi summed up fears that the French accusatorial procedure fostered theatricality and obstructed objective justice:

> To the battle! That is truly the epithet—or rather to the tournament, to the brilliant struggle where, in the sublime exchange of thrusts, in the joyous clink of swords, the grievances that provoked this battle, and those that it

12

will cause, disappear from the eyes of the spectators. . . . The clinic of a theater, rather than a hospital, this courtroom fosters the striking of "attitudes" by virtue of the handsome distances the architect has arranged between the actors. This milieu, this atmosphere, imposes on the personages who will arrive on the brilliant stage from its many entrances, something of the attitude of artists ready to play a role, and already bearing the heat of public scrutiny.[23]

His comment on the theatrical influence of the "belles distances" in the courtroom is particularly revealing. To clarify his argument, he pointed to the criminal courtrooms of the British as a model for French reform, acknowledging that the British had provided the French with the paradigm of oral accusatorial proceedings in the first place. Ironically, he said, the guardians of the accusatorial tradition in London ran matter-of-fact criminal trials in cramped courtrooms, where a grand gesture was unthinkable because the speaker might knock the very wig off a colleague![24] By pointing to the criminal courts at London's Old Bailey, Cruppi argued that it would be possible for France to purge the theatrical excesses of the Cour d'assises and institute proceedings based on the authority of experts without disavowing the principles of publicity and orality.

The criminal courts at Old Bailey provide another example of a complex and delicate relationship between physical and social structuring, which in this case served to diffuse the theatrical potential of orality and publicity (fig. 12). The British gave their criminal courtroom a different orientation, if not a different shape altogether. The modern French courtroom was a long rectangle set up like a basilican Catholic church, so as to maximize the longitudinal axis that culminated in the judges' tribune at the far end of the room. In London, when the courtroom was rectangular rather than square, the judges' bench instead lined the long side of the room, reducing the potential for axial distance and hierarchy beyond the bench. The rest of the room was set up on the model of a Protestant meeting hall, uniting its constituencies rather than splitting them into prosecution and defense.[25] The prisoner occupied a large elevated dock facing the judges, as tall as the bench; sharply graded seating for the jurors and for witnesses lined the side walls between the dock and the bench. At the center of the room were tables (in Cruppi's day, a single table) for defense and prosecution, who sat, Cruppi declared, elbow to elbow, rather than facing one another across the empty space of the French *barreau*. The social paradigm was collegiality, conversation, consensus—not dramatic confrontation. The place of the public in this structure was physically removed: it generally sat in galleries built into the short ends of the room, isolated from the floor but overlooking it—another feature of the meeting-hall type. This was quite different from the situation of the French public, which occupied part of the courtroom proper and participated in the proceedings. Indeed Cruppi praised the phlegmatic British for staging such undramatic trials that the British public generally took little interest in them; he might have added that the British further discouraged public attendance by charging admission, a practice illegal if not unknown in France.[26] Moreover, it is significant that the very concept of resolving the equally cramped conditions in Paris with graded seating and galleries for the public was alien to the French, probably because it would have reduced the symbolic elevation of the bench and the ability of the magistrates to visually survey and police the courtroom—a function accomplished by other means in London.[27]

If the London criminal courtroom was less accusatorial in its physical structure than that of Paris, its procedure, Cruppi argued, was more accusatorial. This reversal was the point of his comparison. Cruppi urged the French to give up their hierarchical distinction between prosecutor and defense lawyer and to adopt the British practice of placing both defense and prosecution at the table before the judge, to argue their cases in a setting of equality. In lieu of the French judge who compromised his ostensible objectivity by personally questioning the defendant and witnesses, Cruppi advocated the British judge, who remained aloof from those proceedings, serving as an impartial umpire. Cruppi realized that evident inequities amidst the promise of balanced debate increased the theatricality of the French courtroom, for it heightened the stakes of courtroom combat. Suspicions and manipulations of suspicions that the contest was unfair justified on the one hand dramatic tactics from the defense and on the other hand repressive assertion of authority by the president, charged with policing the trial. Indeed, the visually chaotic press of bodies in the London courtroom at the particularly sensational Palmer trial of 1856, tolerated by the British, would have posed still graver problems in Paris, where distance and its bridging carried a more obvious political charge and hierarchy in the courtroom was more obviously enforced.[28] It was in this context that Cruppi denounced the vast *barreau* in Paris for encouraging theatricality.

To put Cruppi's observation somewhat differently, it was the very tension between inquisitorial and accusatorial rationales in the French criminal system which escalated theatricality. The political importance of oral debate between the state and the individual was represented by the spacious *barreau*, which encouraged it; the vehemence of that debate and public interest in it rationalized, in turn, the inquisitorial discipline of the presiding judge, who believed himself bound to chasten the abuses of orality, based in part on his privileged knowledge of the case from the dossier on his desk. The president's very attempt to fuse the sovereign will represented in the codes with the will of the live public and jury in his courtroom was apt to arouse their suspicion and resistance. Part of the drama of the French criminal trial, then, was a struggle over authority and its locus.

13. Louis Duc and Honoré Daumet, project for a new place du Palais de Justice, 1869, bird's eye view, looking east, engraving by A. Guillaumot the elder.

Monumental Access

TELLINGLY, the tension between judicial authority and accusatorial procedure was resolved in favor of the latter, due to the political advantage of accommodating publicity, once the location and prominence of the new criminal wing were worked out (fig. 14). In terms of judicial prestige, the criminal courtrooms ought to have been subordinated to the supreme and civil courts in the plan of the Palais. But in the Parisian historic complex, the most prestigious chamber, the civil courtroom of the Supreme Court, was fixed by tradition in an eccentric position, confounding hierarchy. Yet it was not serendipitous that the criminal courts gained the central site behind the new west entrance, additionally linked by monumental corridors to the old entrance at the east.[29] Criminal courts also often got central billing in provincial courthouses, reflecting their social significance. Indeed, in Paris the government intended to make the new criminal wing the main entrance to the Palais, which then became a focus for the prefect

15

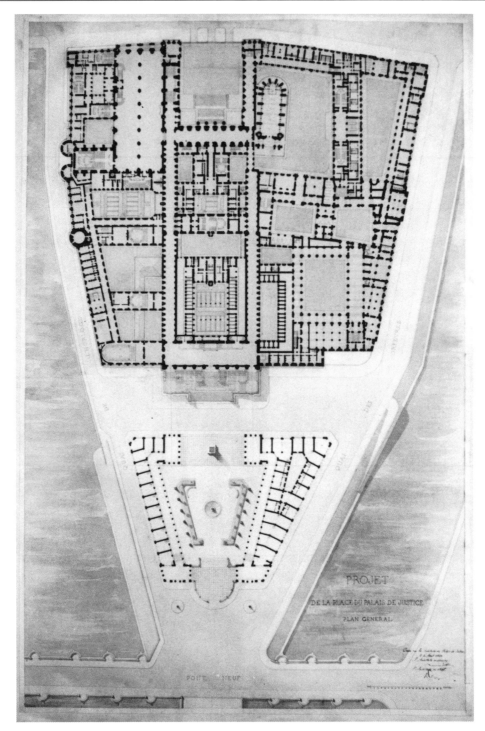

14. Duc and Daumet, project for a new place du Palais de Justice, general plan of the Palais and west end of the Cité, dated August 4, 1869.

Haussmann's replanning of the city. This venture was meant to encompass the 17th-century place Dauphine, a closed triangle of row houses whose original form is shown in the 18th-century Turgot plan of the city roughly as it looked until 1871, screening the old back entrance to the Palais (fig. 16). The Palais architect, Louis Duc, proposed to replace the houses with a low forecourt which would open the Palais to monumental view from the river banks (fig. 13), a project postponed and finally mooted when damage from Paris Commune fires justified the demolition of the houses parallel to the facade, creating the compromise one sees today (fig. 15). Duc's project to replace the place Dauphine would have given the Palais a visibility to match its social importance. Moreover, Haussmann worked to integrate the monument into the new street network unifying the city, plotting early trajectories for the rue de Rennes to improve access from the developing left bank to the pont neuf and the new Palais entrance.[30]

The processional route to the courtroom was all-important. The facade itself formed a kind of sieve, its arcades drawing the public up the grand stair. Peeling back

15. Aerial photograph of the Palais and the île de la Cité, looking east.

16. Detail of the Palais de Justice and the île de la Cité from the plan of Paris for the Prévôt des marchands Turgot, by Bretez, engravings, 1739.

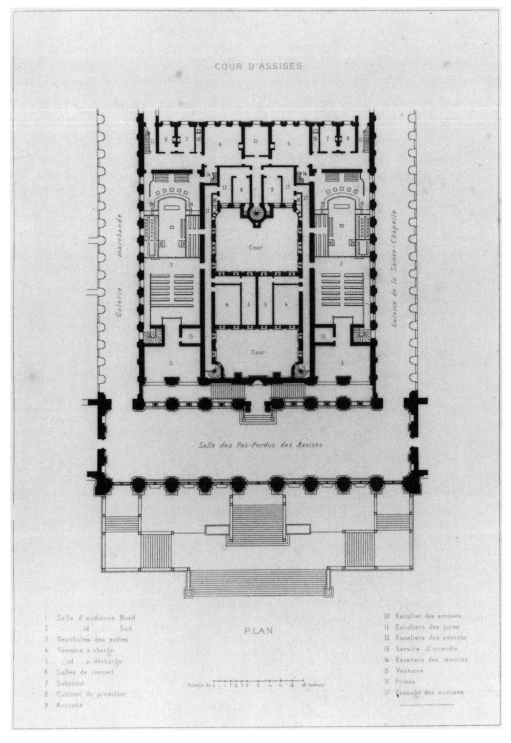

17. Plan of the criminal courts wing, engraving of 1881.

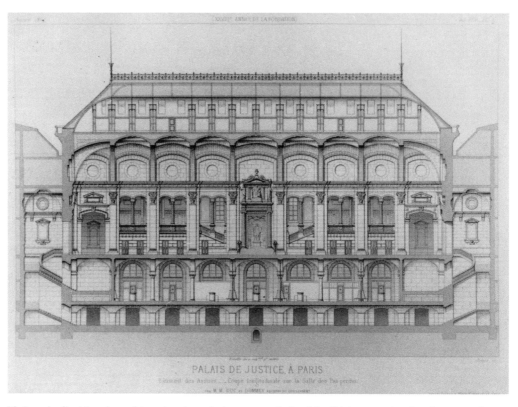

18. Longitudinal (north-south) section through the west vestibule of the Palais, approximating the executed state, engraving, 1867.

layers, one would next enter the vast vaulted vestibule lit by the arcades (fig. 18), and spot the open stairs leading to the pair of criminal courtrooms set at an upper level to leave room for a prison below (fig. 19).[31] Since the new entrance was still obstructed at the time of the Troppmann trial, the public would have taken the old east entrance, and followed one of the long corridors leading west, which hug the courtrooms at the vestibule level (fig. 19). The east entrance, too, gained accessibility in Haussmann's renovation of the plan of Paris, for the boulevard outside was rebuilt as the city's major north-south thoroughfare—the boulevard du Palais linking the boulevard Sébastopol and the boulevard Saint-Michel (fig. 15). This processional route formed another dramatic sequence threading the building from east to west, from the long corridor with its depressed vaults to an explosion of well-lit space, as one turned the corner into the west vestibule, which served as the waiting hall for the courtrooms (figs. 47, 48, 20).[32]

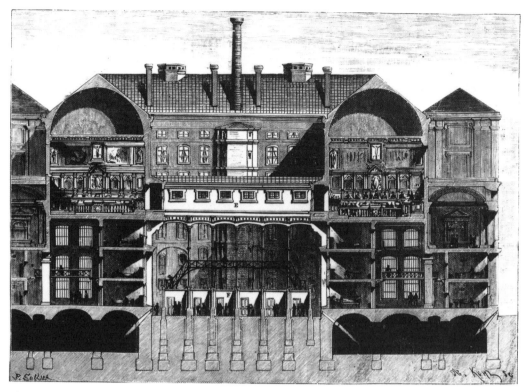

19. Transverse (north-south) section through the criminal courtrooms, looking east, print.

Troppmann's Public

HAVING NOTED the importance of the courtrooms within the Palais and the city, we now turn to the activity within them. Analyzing the actors and proceedings opens a way to understanding not only how the courthouse was used and itself functioned to organize the trial, but ultimately the context and terms in which its architectural character was perceived and judged. We begin with our own counterpart, the 19th-century audience, because it made the trial and courtroom spectacular; my argument will be that the nature of that audience, as construed by 19th-century commentators, had much to do with the construction of the architectural image of justice. The linkage between social practice and material form took place above all through categories of class and gender, which were employed to characterize and explain the public and its behavior, especially to comment on the public's role in the contest between types of authority and modes of procedure discussed above. These social issues are

21

best demonstrated by an inspection of Troppmann's audience, beginning with its sheer size and the question of who actually gained entrance.

The presence of the public was no mere supplement to a modern criminal trial; juridically it was an essential feature, for it fulfilled the principle of publicity established in the codes. But getting into the courtroom at a sensational trial was a challenge, as is evident in a popular illustration of a crowded trial held in the south courtroom in 1872, depicted after the fires set by the Paris Commune in 1871 had destroyed the decoration of the two rooms and before their full restoration (fig. 30). Despite the fact that the new criminal courtroom was much larger than the old one, *(fig. 56)* actually matching the size of the Supreme Court's main chamber, the public complained of lack of space (fig. 56). Standing room between the public entrance and the barrier defining the benches for witnesses could hold a packed crowd of a hundred, for which the public queued for hours. In Troppmann's case, most arrived around 6 a.m. but some camped overnight outside the Palais in the snow to be first in line for the 10:30 trial. Prospective spectators with influence petitioned the presiding judge for an advance invitation that would grant them a seat in the enclosure holding the twelve witness benches. For a trial like Troppmann's, the architects adjusted the benches to fit in extras, creating about one hundred fifty cramped places for Paris society. In practice, some of the privileged spectators proved adept at infiltrating the *barreau* itself, which offered incomparably better vantage points on the proceedings (fig. 28). The limitation of two hundred fifty spectators left a large and disappointed crowd milling in the hall outside, the vestibule de Harlay, where it awaited news of the proceedings at court recesses—as seen in a sketch made during the Pranzini trial of 1887 (fig. 20). Some measure of the crowds (and official expectations for them) can be gleaned from the size of the civil and military police forces deployed to control them: two hundred municipal sergeants to oversee the east entrance to the Palais and a detachment of the military police or Paris Guard to line the corridors from the east entrance to the criminal waiting hall and stairs.[33]

In effect, a two-class system of access to the courtroom operated during most of the century, and the class identity of the public (as well as the defendant) was an important factor in discussions of criminal justice. As a court reporter declared in a retrospective comment:

> The public is clearly divided: on the reserved seats there is lace, here in back are blue handkerchiefs; up in front is the scent of heliotrope, back here, the stench of garlic sausage.[34]

Interest in trials like Troppmann's pervaded—and even united—the spectrum of classes. Demand for tickets was as intense as that for standing room. The fabulous estimate of the number of ticket requests at 15,000 attests to the celebrity of the affair.[35] The paper *Le Droit* declared that the bribes offered to judicial staff for tickets

L'AFFAIRE PRANZINI. — Aspect de la salle des Pas-Perdus, au Palais-de-Justice, pendant le procès.
[Dessin de M. Marc Aurèle.]

20. West vestibule during the Pranzini trial of 1887, print based on sketch by Marc Aurèle.

would surely exceed the price of admission to the most sought-after plays. Successful petitioners included numerous legislative deputies, such as the duc de Mouchy, an aristocrat who had recently married into the imperial family, and the marquis de Guilloutet, who had ironically won notoriety by authoring article 11 of the 1868 press law barring newspapers from reporting details of private life; Maxime Du Camp, whose investigative reportage of Paris institutions in the *Revue des deux mondes* was attracting attention; the art critic and writer, Arsène Houssaye; the popular playwrights Emile Augier, Adolphe Dennery, and Alexandre Dumas the younger, of whom the latter had recently published a novel about a criminal case; as well as several celebrated actors and singers, such as the Opéra's Madame Carvalho-Miolan. Tickets, however, were rumored to pass from approved to less "respectable" hands by the time of the trial, accounting for a number of popular actresses and courtesans amid the allegedly high proportion of female spectators. A passion for trials also led to crossover between classes in the standing room area. Unsuccessful petitioners for tickets resorted to purchasing places at the front of the queue for standing room, places that fetched, according to the press, prices ranging from 500 to thousands of francs. Society overcame class and gender scruples to squeeze among the *peuple* at the back of the courtroom.[36]

The two-tier system of admission reflected professional ambivalence about the public—both the idle poor and the idle rich. The ticket system was not mandated in the code of criminal procedure, but arose as a custom soon after the Cour d'assises was established; challenged in petitions to the Cour de cassation, it was upheld as a legitimate exercise of the virtually unlimited powers of the president, specified in the code, to maintain order in his courtroom. In explaining this, Justice Nouguier did not specify why limiting the unreserved seating on a first-come first-served basis was inadequate to maintain order, but the Third Republic's Paris Assises president Bérard des Glajeux characterized the issue as one of class.[37] Fears ran high about the motives of the public-at-large; the president could screen those who sat in the reserved area, but could only speculate on the motives of those at the back, identifiable by their clothing as working class. Despite the growing tendency to distinguish a virtuous *classe laborieuse* from the *classe dangereuse* represented by criminal defendants generally from poor backgrounds (an effort that we shall see in practice in the Troppmann trial debates), suspicion persisted that working class spectators were likely to be in league with the defendant.[38] Du Camp maintained that they included thieves, who stopped by to instruct themselves in judicial workings; President Bérard declared that friends and accomplices of guilty defendants tended to pack the standing area and sway the actors in the trial with their responses. Significantly, Bérard worried more about audience responsiveness—that is, the "turbulence" in the courtroom caused by the lack of "conditions de déférence et de dépendance" among an unscreened working class audience—than about the security risk that partisans might aid the defendant to escape.[39]

But even the highly select group deemed suitable for tickets was suspect, because it too was responsive—perhaps more so because it could see and hear better and could talk with the witnesses who joined it on the benches after testifying. Bérard described the public on the benches thus:

> They had their own values, traditions, jurisprudence, their own independent point of view, and acted effectively either to control the impressions of the press, or to alert the jurors, always very sensitive to the reactions of their counterparts among the public, to any hint of courtroom incidents. They constituted a second, external jury.[40]

A series of ministers of justice similarly warned the magistrature that the privileged public was especially dangerous:

> Individuals unfamiliar with judicial customs, avid for emotion, seeking above all to satisfy their curiosity, have been allowed to sit in the enclosed

area. This is a veritable abuse: those who crowd into the enclosed area at a major trial make the policing of the courtroom difficult and may distract the witnesses. It may even be feared that the sentiments that this crowd expresses for or against the accused could affect the jury and influence its verdicts.[41]

To that statement from 1844, another minister added in 1887:

This custom . . . risks altering the character which ought to mark all judicial hearings, and thus will mar the dignity of justice; it can also expose magistrates to unfair criticism.[42]

What the judges wanted was a silent public audience; contemporary press coverage of trials confirms their complaint that even the elite public was never passive, for journalists' transcriptions of official proceedings were regularly punctuated with reports of audience response, an extended version of the notations of the deputies' "rires" and "murmures" scattered through newspaper reports (once reinstated) of legislative debates. The public appears to have considered itself a participant in the trial, and insisted on judging the evidence and coming to its own conclusions; the juridical tenet that criminal justice lent itself to lay judgment by a jury drawn from the public supported the old Revolutionary notion that justice was in fact done in the name of the French, rather than of Louis-Napoléon, to whom the Second Empire magistrature had sworn allegiance.

Underlying the dispute over the role of the public was the clash of two fundamental ideological principles. On the one hand, there survived the principle of the ancien régime monarchy that justice inhered in the person of the ruler and flowed from him to his people, through his delegates, the magistrature; the function of exercising justice was indeed one of the justifications for kingship. That the king merely delegated justice to his judges was evident in the fact that he retained the power to revise or forestall sentences; he was the judge of last resort. On the other hand, the Revolution had established the republican principle that sovereignty and hence justice were based in the people, and (temporarily) eliminated the right of pardon. In order to make the magistrature responsible to the sovereign will, exemplified by written law, the Revolution also established the corollary principle that magistrates should implement justice independent of executive government. But Napoléon I permanently compromised that doctrine of the separation of powers by stipulating that the executive government would appoint the magistrature. This cast doubt on the tenet that the magistrature served a sovereign people rather than an individual ruler.

From whom justice emanated was one of the contested issues of volatile French politics in the 19th century, and the persistent representation of justice as lodged in the disembodied texts of the codes during the first half of the century did not settle the matter. The Bourbon Restoration and the July Monarchy had decreed that justice emanated once more from the sacred person of the king; the Second Republic formally returned justice to the sovereign people. The Second Empire left the matter ambiguous, providing that while Louis-Napoléon was responsible to the French people, he delegated the right to pronounce justice in his name to his magistrates, and he remained the court of last resort, retaining the right to pardon. (He put his mark on the courtroom as well, indirectly through the motif of the Napoleonic eagle and initial N in the wall-covering above the panelling, and explicitly through the bust mounted on the wall above the dock—a portrait over which the administration took great pains.) Thus political experience, and specifically Louis-Napoléon's compromise, opened a breach in that judicial premise, discussed above, that the magistrature dominated the public in its courtroom so as to infuse that unruly sample of the public with the sovereign universal will inscribed in the Napoleonic codes. When in doubt as to the interests of the magistrature or, indeed, the code, the public declared its sovereignty.[43]

From this difference over the locus of authority followed a difference in basis for judgment. Public judgment followed a different, though legally prescribed, course from professional judgment. Even though the public had access to findings from the pretrial investigation through the popular newspapers, it reacted above all to how the case was represented live in court—whereas it was the magistrate's job to prepare and direct the trial proceedings on the basis of first-hand knowledge of the written dossier from the investigation. And as we shall see when considering the jury, response based on impressions of performance was explicitly stipulated in the code as the basis for lay judgment of criminal cases. The behavior of the public attests to the dynamics of oral story-telling, as Ong summarizes them, rather than those of a document-based procedure. It is precisely those features typical of oral communication that worried magistrates: the way the audience reacted immediately to the statements of a witness or lawyer, for instance, influenced that witness or lawyer to tailor his or her comments to that audience. Moreover, live presentation, as we have noted, tended to foster surprise evidence, which the audience picked up instantly. While jurors were part of the same lay constituency, they were disciplined by an iron-clad rule not to reveal their reactions in their expressions or their questions; the audience response characteristic of oral procedure was thus left to the public. In short, the magistrates supposed that evidence existed as a thing in itself and its persuasiveness depended on its apparent objective integrity, while for the latter 19th-century public, evidence was effectively contextual and discursive. Both systems, of course, accommodated manipulation, but these politics were articulated mainly by the magistrature, whose perspective provides insight into the contestation of authority between them.[44]

Dynamic audience response was condemned by magistrates and proponents of judicial authority as emotional rather than reasoned. It was suspect because, by its apparent spontaneity, it seemed to escape that intellectual process by which reason was now supposed to intervene to organize and discipline sense impressions through language and its logic. Jan Goldstein's analysis of early 19th-century definitions of insanity and its treatment in France suggests a certain tension between the concepts of reason and of sense impressions within Condillac's pervasive formulation of reason as grounded in sense impressions. As construed by the influential doctor Pinel, following Condillac, insanity entailed a deregulated prelinguistic imagination, over-sensitive to impressions, in which the disciplining function of reason and language had to be reinstated. Insofar as the language employed in trials was an oral one informed by gesture and expression, which appealed to the imagination, that language (speech or *parole*, rather than *langue*) posed certain challenges to a persistent Enlightenment model of rational reflection.[45]

Suspicion of oral evidence and its judgment was expressed most clearly in criticism of the presence and conduct of women at the trial, especially in the elite audience. For contemporary commentators on criminal justice, gender was as important as class in defining the public. Newspaper reporters, general observers, and judges alike condemned what they described as a striking percentage of women, with an unseemly zeal for criminal trials. As Du Camp put it, "the supposed sensitivity that women are fond of claiming for themselves hardly accords with such a fierce and unhealthy curiosity" as they demonstrate in the courtroom. A reporter for the popular *Petit journal* agreed:

> Isn't it strange, that mad, unbridled passion shown by women raised in velvets, lace, and silk, accustomed to vapid sentimentality, trivialities, and frivolity, who fall into a faint over nothing . . . for the coarse details and repugnant debates so typical of criminal cases![46]

Such fascination with crime was said to reveal the essential emotionalism of female nature, that is, its susceptibility to emotion and sensation without the higher discipline of reason.[47] It was convenient to explain this worrisome fascination with oral courtroom drama, which clearly pervaded both sexes, by transferring it to the female members of the audience. A reporter for the *Gazette des tribunaux* acknowledged that the responses of women were also shared by men, but came to the conclusion that men disciplined themselves as women could not:

> One can understand, in the circumstances of the trial, the often violent and irresistible expansion of feeling which is natural to men, but perhaps even more natural in women.

For this reason, the reporter continued, President Thévenin was to be lauded for having, in the Troppmann trial, restricted women with tickets to the back of the reserved area, for femininity constituted the opposite of masculine, reasoned justice:

It must be admitted that the presence of elegant well-dressed ladies at the very feet of the judges' bench, near the box of Messieurs the jurors, not far from the accused, is always rather shocking. It gives the character of an indiscrete and worldly spectacle to the grave and severe manifestations of justice.[48]

Female curiosity and unbridled determination, however, overcame the president's orders, according to Du Camp, who reported that "les filles célèbres du mauvais monde parisien, les actrices du renom" found their way into the *barreau*; worse yet, they expressed their views about the case by wearing black, which prejudiced the impartiality of the hearing and surely also camouflaged them among the mass of black-robed lawyers whose benches they infiltrated.[49] Indeed Du Camp's attribution of the conditions of undesirable "spectacle" in the courtroom especially to actresses underscores a set of associations among femininity, class, orality, and its theatrical aspect.

It is significant that even public reporters and commentators like Du Camp dissimulated or condemned their own participation in courtroom response, which they often deemed theatrical. The claim that the public transformed the trial into theater deserves particular attention, for it focuses the larger question of what a public event like a trial was supposed to accomplish. We have already noted how the oral trial was construed as a spectacle which appealed directly to sensations and emotions and hence as a form of theater, and why that theatrical aspect was considered suspect. Another form of pejorative comparison of the courtroom to the theater rested less on absolute mistrust of that kind of theater than on decorum. Some observers invoked the theater explicitly while others drew analogies to other places of still less constrained public activity, such as the market and the waiting hall of the train station.[50] These comparisons contrasted the gravity of criminal charges and their penalties to the bustle and air of excitement among the public. For instance, spectators were wont to bring picnic hampers and even champagne to fortify themselves during recesses in day-long proceedings, when they dared not leave their seats for fear of losing them; worse yet, said commentators, was the commercial hawking of refreshments in the courtroom. That aspect of life as usual, especially the comforts of life, struck critics as unseemly in a criminal courtroom where life hung precisely in the balance. Moreover, spectators tended to dress elegantly, expecting to be observed themselves—creating embarrassment that such wealth and self-display, attributed to women, attended the judgment of generally impoverished defendants. Most damningly, the analogy implied that spectators were treating the trial as an entertainment for themselves, distancing themselves from the debate between the rights of the defendant and those of society, and thereby evading application of its stern moral lesson to their own lives. Finally, 19th-century concern with the basis of theatrical interaction and with decorum points to another issue: a construction of the purpose of the courtroom as anti-theatrical, or as about the unmasking of imposters. Many commentators compared not only the public but all the non-magistrates in the trial—the defendant, the lawyer, and even the witnesses—to actors, predisposed to subterfuge, and construed the court's role as to distinguish play-acting from truth. An audience disposed to enjoy a good performance was not liable to seek to undermine its own pleasure.

At stake here was the extension of a critique of theatricality developed by Enlightenment playwrights and critics, most notably Diderot. The Second Empire courtroom effectively evoked 18th-century theaters in which royalty and aristocratic dandies actually sat on the stage—like the elite audience in the *barreau* and behind the judges—and felt free to converse among themselves, or to address the voluble audience standing in the *parterre*, or to interact with the actors of classical French plays. Pejorative comparison of trial to theater extended Enlightenment condemnation of that elite audience for self-display and interference with the actors and the play—characteristics the Enlightenment coded as feminine—and ultimately for an autonomy that supported its lack of identification with the actors and their story.[51] The comparison also evoked the 19th-century theaters on the so-called "boulevard du crime," where the well-to-do enjoyed mingling with popular audiences to watch melodramatic spectacles not unlike criminal trials; such promiscuous mixing of publics, especially voluble ones, raised governmental anxiety about risk to social order. That worry was eased in 1862 when the city demolished most of those theaters as part of its program of urban renewal, but at least one survived to perpetuate the genre, the Théâtre de la Porte-Saint-Martin.[52] And the aspect of gay luxury and self-display observed in the courtroom was a constituent feature of the chief official venue for *grand spectacle* in Paris, as it was being rebuilt by the Second Empire: the Opéra.[53] Clearly the critique of theatricality so firmly launched in the Enlightenment had not eliminated its target, though it continued to promote an alternate mode of spectacle, which the magistrature considered more appropriate to the courtroom: the *drame bourgeois* formulated by Diderot and others, designed to induce silent contemplation from an audience drawn to identify with its characters and their moral lessons. Yet the spectacle of self-sacrifice or voluntary return to virtue in the face of temptation proved difficult to draw from frequently non-bourgeois defendants accused of capital crimes, and melodramatic confrontations of vice with virtue, like those of the boulevard theaters, tended instead to dominate trials like Troppmann's. In a melodramatic scenario, characteristic of oral story-telling, the impulse to participate overwhelmed the public's will to demonstrate a normative self-discipline.[54]

From a historical perspective, the theatrical metaphor is ironic in two significant respects. First, it has been argued that middle- and upper-class theater audiences became increasingly silent and passive by the 1870s, abandoning the practice of energetic response that characterized past theater, whereas the full range of lay participants in the courtroom grew increasingly assertive.[55] Secondly, commentators, even while condemning the excitement of the courtroom public as frivolous, acknowledged paradoxically that its intensity was due precisely to the awareness that the trial had real-life consequences.[56] Not surprisingly in that period of positivism and of realist programs and criticism in the arts, the public seems to have shared, however diffusely, in a general sense of an epistemological split between "reality" and representations of it, which needs to be considered as part of the subject of social representations of institutions such as justice at this period. To dismiss the volatility of the public in the courtroom as simply frivolous was in itself disingenuous, for the public's responsiveness seems rather to have followed from engagement in its role as participant in an oral performance—a role especially familiar to the women in the audience.

This conflict over the very nature of the public even infused discussion of the appropriate response from authorities. On the one hand, publicity was a condition of post-Revolutionary democratic ideology, which was conveniently treated as a didactic means to reinforce social values among the public and deter criminal impulses;[57] on the other hand, it was said to foster mobocracy, swaying the jury from impartiality by its volatile and wayward responses.[58] These fears served to justify the broad discretionary powers of the president to police the courtroom and restrain the atmosphere of fête; they also rationalized the limited public area and its placement toward the back of a long, narrow room, a circumstance that not only limited but also distanced the public and provoked intense complaint about the difficulty of seeing and hearing.[59] Interestingly, it was the privileged public entrusted with seats in the courtroom proper that was curtailed towards the end of the century. When in 1891, the minister of justice abolished reserved seating and banished Paris society to the rear of the room with the poor, President Bérard protested, comparing the measure to the authoritarian barring of the public from the legislature during the Second Empire.[60]

The rights of two specialized sectors of the audience to seats in the *barreau* remained uncontested, however, even in 1891: the professional audience of lawyers and magistrates who wished simply to observe the trial (or those moments at which their colleagues made their major performances), and journalists reporting on the trial. Some 40 lawyers packed onto the lawyers' benches edging the *barreau*—and sometimes even appropriated the defendant's dock; magistrates, accompanied by such foreign diplomats as the Russian ambassador, treated as special guests of the government, crowded onto the platform behind the judges' bench. While their presence surely encouraged virtuosic performances on the part of the trial magistrates and lawyers, their behavior was chastened by a shared professional protocol.

Professional reputations were more likely to be made by the judicial press, which had a special place of its own in the *barreau*: a box adjacent to the jury's box, facing the defendant (fig. 56). The high partition separating the press from the jurors, of which the press complained, effectively sequestered the jury from the press and from easy visual contact with the public. But the very provision of a press box in the new

behind !

courtroom was an innovation journalists applauded, especially as it afforded writing surfaces for their notes, and its placement clearly indicated the role of the press as the logical extension of the jury and the effective representative of the public, to whom it diffused its findings. Indeed, in the case of the non-juried misdemeanors courts in Paris, the press literally took the place that the jury held in the criminal courts, and in the criminal courtroom in the twentieth century, when the jury began to sit with the magistrates at the judges' bench, expressing a change in its role, the press took over its box. Yet at Troppmann's trial, the press box proved inadequate; the normally Parisian press swelled with provincial and international colleagues. One journalist expanded their force further with the claim that each represented a public of 20,000 readers outside the courtroom. Moreover, President Thévenin's decision to restrict tickets for reserved seats to use for a single day of the trial allowed the press to declare that it represented true publicity, for of the possible publics, it alone had first-hand knowledge of the entire trial. These specialized publics completed the crowd in the courtroom, forming, in the words of the *Petit journal*, a human garland around the empty space in the *barreau* where the proceedings would take place.[61]

The Trial Personae: Choreography and Character

WITH SPECTATORS installed, those with professional roles in the trial began to arrive, through that array of specialized staircases and entrances from the backstage dependencies to which Cruppi derogatorily referred. Indeed, this was the means of entry even for those lawyers and judges who attended as spectators. The complexity of this choreography is evident in the plan of the courtroom, which reveals no less than seven entrances (fig. 17). This plan, excerpted from that of the rest of the Palais in order to explicate the special services of the criminal courts in a 19th-century publication, shows how the Cour d'assises was conceived as a self-enclosed package of public areas and private dependencies compacted into a hollow rectangle and dropped into place between the two monumental corridors linking the east and west entrances, and above the ground-floor prison (figs. 18, 19, 21). The lofty courtrooms themselves stretch to either side of a prison exercise yard concealed at the center; the cross-sections show the blind arcades of their inner walls lining the courtyard, above the gridwork of small openings into the cell blocks below (figs. 19, 21, 22). While the public enters those courtrooms from the end adjoining the great waiting hall, other participants in the trial enter at the opposite end, from a private several-story wing of offices and deliberation chambers connecting the courtrooms at the rear, or from the private stairs linking the courtroom to the flanking east-west corridor.

Most striking is the distinction between the entrances for magistrates and for

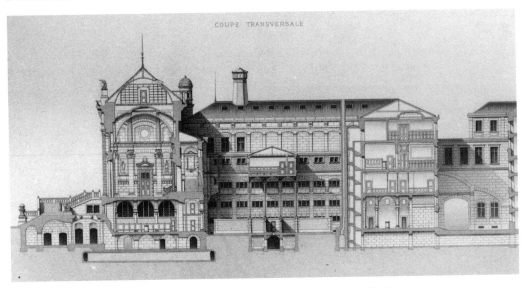

21. Transverse (east-west) section through the criminal courts wing, engraving of 1881.

22. View of the internal courtyard of the criminal courts wing, looking north, showing the individualized exercise yards of the prison, with the witnesses' chambers carried above them on colonnettes, engraving of 1881.

lawyers, since this ceremonial difference announced and symbolized the difference in status and style between the two sides of the case. Lawyers entered from the public or west end of the courtroom, but arrived from a private stairway tucked to the side of the courtroom's public doors (#12 on the plan in fig. 17), and traversed a private passageway lining one side of the witnesses' enclosure to reach their own bench below the dock in the *barreau*. They arrived in costume, having donned their black robes and hats or *toques* in a lawyers' vestiary in another part of the Palais. This was in contrast to the majestic entrance of the magistrates, from the doorways behind the bench at the opposite end of the room. Both the prosecutor and the presiding judge had offices directly behind the courtroom (#7 and #8) and the three judges and the prosecutor and his assistants used the robing room (#15) to dress in the costume that judge and prosecutor shared, indicating their common status as magistrates: a red robe with white fur trim, as well as the *toque*. These red robes were not merely more splendid than the black garb of lawyers, they literally signified royal authority, for traditionally high-ranking magistrates had received their red robes as hand-me-downs from the king and wore them at the king's funeral to signify the immortality of sovereignty. In this sense red-robed magistrates made a competing bid for sovereignty not only with lawyers, but also with the spectators and jurors whose public status was signified by their lack of uniform. Magistrates had two doorways: a simple service one at the right end of the rear wall, leading to their offices, and a monumental one crowned with lions, at right angles to it, bearing an inscription identifying it as the gateway to the deliberation chamber. Announced by an usher's rap on these doors and the cry "La cour, messieurs!," at which all in the courtroom rose and removed their hats, the magistrates processed slowly to their armchairs on the judicial tribune, further distinguishing the shared elevated status of judges and prosecutors from the lawyers in the *barreau* below them. That loud noise and the magistrates' introduction as a single corporate body demarcated the time and space of the trial as a ritual presided by magistrates, who would seek to subsume the individual identities of all those in the courtroom into the roles of trial participants, and prompt those actors to acquiesce in the social order that the magistrature represented.[62]

The magisterial status of the prosecutor expressed the prominence of that post in the French judicial system. French jurists frequently reiterated that France had invented the very office of public prosecutor, later adapted by other nations. As in the ancien régime, the prosecutor represented society as construed by the executive government. Formerly the representative of the sovereign king's interests, the post-Revolutionary prosecutor was the untenured agent of the executive government's Ministry of Justice. In criminal affairs, he saw to it that the lower-ranking, untenured examining magistrate, or *juge d'instruction*, who carried out the pretrial investigation took the ministry's instructions seriously; independent-minded *juges d'instruction* could be fired or barred from promotions. The prosecutor then represented the results of that inquisitorial investigation at the public trial. In Troppmann's case, the importance that the government placed on the case and its verdict was immediately evident in the fact that the chief prosecutor himself, the Procureur général Grandperret, appeared as well as his deputy, the avocat général, who normally represented the prosecution in the criminal courts. The ministry picked its chief prosecutor partly for his proven ability to sway juries, and, in this case, Grandperret would have to counteract the leading criminal defense lawyer of the day, the celebrated Lachaud.[63]

The professional bonds between prosecutor and judges were obvious to the public, even though these two types of magistrates differed in political status. Maxime du Camp had just reiterated, in the well-read *Revue des deux mondes*, the Napoleonic principle that (even though judges were appointed by the executive government and swore allegiance to it) judges were tenured in order to guarantee their impartiality, unlike the prosecutors. This was the standard statement on the subject. Yet a recent reform tract by Prévost-Paradol had called public attention to the inadequacy of tenure, pointing out how judges depended on satisfying the government to receive promotions, for which, he said, the presidency of the Cour d'assises was a stepping stone.[64] In fact, judges depended on recommendations from prosecutors for promotions, and the presiding judge for criminal trials generally was selected by the chief prosecutor from among the judges of the appellate court. Insiders knew further that in terms of professional hierarchy and income, as well as actual power, the prosecutor ranked above the presiding judge, even though the president exercised, as the *Petit Journal* briefed its readers before the Troppmann trial, "the most important role during the debates of a criminal trial." The newspaper referred not only to the president's job of directing the trial and personally questioning its participants, but also to his unlimited discretionary powers to maintain order in the courtroom. All this amounted to considerable symbolic and actual authority for the magistrature, linked to the will of the government. Although the professional ethos of a magistrate, prosecutors included, demanded a degree of "*réserve*" or apparent impartiality unexpected of lawyers, the public felt compelled to keep watch on the president for signs of undue partisanship.[65]

The lay actors, jurors and witnesses, were called forward and differentiated from the public to assume their special status at the start of the trial. However, witnesses sat with the invited public until the proceedings began, while jurors were singled out even before the defendant arrived in the courtroom. That process had its own architectural choreography with several steps, from the reduction of the pool of forty jurors for the two-week session to a twelve-man jury for the particular trial, to the swearing-in of that judgment jury at its station in the jury box.

To what extent did that pool of session jurors represent the unrestricted public-at-large watching from the back of the courtroom? This question raises further questions—not merely the social make-up of the jury, but how it was selected and by what principle of sovereignty. Was this lay jury constituted or perceived as a jury of peers that represented the sovereign people, and if so, in what sense? The representational basis of the jury was an explosive political issue constantly reformulated during the 19th century. For debate over who would judge affected laymen as well as professionals. Just as the make-up and permanence of the magistrature was thrown into question under each new regime, so too the laws for jury service were continually revised. The law established at the beginning of the Second Empire marked an ideological change in the government's definition of the jury, and one that came in for resistance from jurors themselves, as well as from critics of the regime during its liberal phase at the time of Troppmann's trial.

The Second Empire inherited the principle that jury service was a political right which expressed and guaranteed popular sovereignty by effecting popular representation in the criminal courts, as in the legislature. If preceding constitutional monarchies, which reinvested judicial sovereignty in kings, had restricted this republican principle by limiting the right to vote and to serve on a jury to men with a minimum of property or income, the Second Republic had expanded it in 1848 to all male adults regardless of wealth. The Empire moved quickly to reject the very principle of that law. Conserving the form of universal suffrage, the imperial legislature nonetheless passed a new jury selection law in 1853, formally declaring that jury service was not a political right (*un droit*) but a service (*fonction*) which required particular intellectual and moral capabilities. On these grounds, the 1853 law reformed the selection process. The previous Republican law of 1848 had, it is true, eschewed the proposal to draw the jury by lot directly from voter lists; instead, it specified that *elected* officials choose an annual list of prospective jurors from the local electorate as the basis for a lottery that yielded forty names for each session of criminal trials. The 1853 law separated that annual list from the voter list; moreover, it decreed that government-appointed officials would choose local men whom they considered trustworthy. Property remained irrelevant. But since jury service was unremunerated, workers were legally exempt and therefore rarely even included on the annual lists, and well-to-do entrepreneurs frequently excused themselves. Socially, Second Empire jurors were dominated by petty bourgeois in commerce, with smaller proportions of men of private means and from the liberal professions, all of whom local government officials could certify as "intelligent, ethical, [and] supporters of law and order."[66] They were not to consider themselves representatives of the sovereign public, but rather, servants of a sovereign system of law and order. There is even evidence that the government exercised police surveillance over prospective jurors, and (illegally) attempted to document the vote of individual jurors, so as to be certain of its men.[67] Thus, the Empire endeavored in theory and in practice to separate the jury from the public at large.

We have already heard the president Bérard declare that the criminal courtroom contained two different juries, the official jury and the public. But Bérard's comment and our inspection of that second jury, the public audience, equally indicate how energetically the public competed with the magistrature for the loyalty of the official jury. In practice, even so carefully selected a group as the Second Empire jury was notorious among magistrates for its independence. Citing magistrates' reports as well as statistics, Second Empire ministers of justice—even Ollivier—complained of juries' lenient verdicts, blaming them for rising rates of recidivism, and, by 1868, for an alarming increase in crime. On the other hand, liberals at the time of Troppmann's trial demanded a reform of jury selection which would generate even greater jury independence from magisterial influence.[68] This situation meant that the ritual by which the jury was brought forward from the public and invested with responsibility was critical for shaping its temporary identity. The steps in this ritual literally situated the jury in a world suspended between the lay public and the magistrature.

The first step took place out of the public eye, in the magistrates' domain. For the selection of the judgment jury, session jurors followed the judges back out of the courtroom through the lion-crowned doorway to the judicial deliberation chamber.[69] There the president drew names from the urn figured in Cour d'assises iconography, with rights of rejection by the watching prosecution and defense. In this setting, jurors again confronted the grandeur of the magistrature, for the judicial chamber was more splendid than the jury's lower-ceilinged rooms up a ladder-like staircase (fig. 21). From an initial meeting, the session jury was familiar with the quarters reserved for themselves; members knew to take the private entrance for jurors in the east-west corridor, and climb the stair leading on the first floor to the jurors' door into the courtroom, to one side of the judges' bench, and on the second floor to the jurors' suite of kitchen, dining room and deliberation chamber, where jurors could dine during recesses in the lengthy proceedings, isolated from temptations to discuss the case with non-jurors. But journalists and magistrates interpreted the relegation of jurors to the attic, and the contrast of their plain quarters to the magistrates' chamber, enhanced by ceiling paintings and sculpture, as indications of status. Relative status was underlined in the ceremony of jury selection, where judges and prosecutors sat in armchairs at the central table, while the jurors and the accused and his counsel stood at the margins, equally intruders on the magistrates' sanctuary. This was the jury's first encounter with the defendant, and Cruppi argued that the contrast between the prosecution and the defense, and indeed between the red-robed judge and the civilian juror was enough to align the jurors with the defendant. For Bérard, on the other hand, the grandeur of the magistrature placed it above the fray, and inspired the jurors to emulation. Facing the jurors from above the fireplace was the bust of the presiding judge of the early 17th-century Paris courts, Achille de Harlay, the namesake of the rue de Harlay and of the western vestibule and waiting hall, the vestibule de Harlay—in Bérard's words, "the image of a moderate in troubled times, well chosen to inspire impartiality and firmness in jurors with a sense of history."[70]

It was only on returning to the courtroom that the jurors took their official position in the *barreau*. The judgment jury entered through its own door and corridor at one side of the judges' bench, narrowly skirting the armchair of the prosecutor on the way to its box, facing the defendant. In that accusatorial confrontation with the defendant, the jury was aligned with the prosecutor, whose chair on the judicial tribune above was observed to overhang the jury box; the foreman, who would direct the jury deliberation, took the seat closest to the prosecutor's. But if the layout of the courtroom implied a certain alliance, even subordination, between jury and prosecutor, it also differentiated between the lay and professional judges by setting the jury at right angles to the bench. Similar to the location of American juries, this arrangement nonetheless underscored the difference considered so problematic in 19th-century France between the prerogatives of juries, supposed to determine guilt without thought for the sentence, and judges, responsible for pronouncing the legal penalty. In 1941, when the French decided that such a separation between lay and professional activity was unenforceable, French jurors began to sit with the judges at the bench, but in the 19th century, distinctions and mutual suspicions were marked.[71]

The oath by which the jurors were sworn in as temporary judges evidenced that problematic relationship. On the one hand, this ritual was celebrated as a magical moment in the proceedings, the transmutation of private individuals into public servants, and of private affairs into public ones.[72] The stature of invested jurors was acknowledged by the fact that they and the lawyers were the only non-magistrates in the courtroom with the legal right to wear their hats—a symbol of honor whose history of mortal significance has recently been pointed out by Natalie Zemon Davis.[73] Yet the oath itself specified the non-professional manner in which the jurors were to judge: "suivant votre conscience et votre intime conviction." What this meant was amplified by article 342 of the code of criminal procedure posted in the jury rooms:

> The law does not ask jurors to explain how they reach their decision, nor does it prescribe rules for assessing the extent and sufficiency of a piece of evidence. It tells them to search their consciences in silent meditation for the impression that the proofs presented against and for the accused have made upon their minds. The law does not say: "You must take as true every fact attested by a certain number of witnesses;" nor: "You must reject as insufficient every ostensible proof that does not consist of a particular number or particular types of evidence;" the law asks but one question which sums up the entire responsibility of the jurors: "Have you an *intime conviction*?"[74]

To describe the juror's job in negative terms is clearly reactive, and these instructions, dating from the code of 1808, represented a reaction against pre-Revolutionary inquisitorial practice in criminal courts, in which the judge's discretionary power to determine the sentence was counterbalanced by strict rules of evidence and methods of calculating the admissibility and weight of various types of "legal proofs," in which the judge's personal convictions had little place. The modern criminal system purported to remove legal expertise from the judgment of evidence, distinguishing between judges of law—the professional judges who applied the penalties as specified in the code, and judges of fact—the jurors. In place of rules of evidence, the code prescribed a moral basis for the judgment of fact.

This change in the nature of judgment and judge was predicated on the change in the evidence in question—the shift from a document-based procedure to an oral, accusatorial trial. Nouguier specified these connections in explaining how the jury reached an *intime conviction* by assessing the moral credibility of the accused and of witnesses, through visual scrutiny of their performance, in tandem with their statements (fig. 31, upper left hand vignette). He wrote of witnesses, for instance:

> Oral debate is the fundamental, absolute rule—and, I would add, a necessity. Without it, the institution of the jury would be meaningless in principle and impossible in practice. For the jury, the entrance of a witness, his physiognomy, his bearing, his tone of voice, are so many reasons for confidence or doubt. A word, a gesture, a look, a feeling obviously suppressed, embarrassment poorly dissimulated, an involuntary movement of distress or indignation, all can serve—in the midst of interpolations and revealing contradictions—to bare the secret thought of the witness. Suppress all that, or rather, substitute the cold analysis of the dossier, or an even colder reading of the documents or the written depositions within it, and you will deprive the jury of those moral elements, those living proofs, by which the juror, fulfilling his oath, enlightens his conscience and forms his *intime conviction.*[75]

Thus the criminal court was legally constituted as a jurisdiction of impressions, to use the phrase of one veteran juror, meaning that jurors were required to work as much with visual and aural impressions as with the content of what was said in the debates.[76] This was precisely that aspect of orality that some contemporaries compared pejoratively to "spectacle" and "theater," drawing on a discourse of skepticism about the authenticity of performance and appearance initiated in the 18th century; yet in the courtroom it constituted the legal, explicitly non-professional basis for the professed goal of unmasking truth.[77]

If the techniques of professionals' examinations of their subject have been theorized in terms of the authoritative gaze, the jury's lay examination was equally visual.[78] The nature of the jury's work was expressed, for instance, in the unilateral lighting of the room, considered an essential aspect of latter 19th-century criminal courtroom design.[79] The jury sat below large clerestory windows which illuminated the dock and highlit the defendant's every movement; the jury itself remained in shadow (fig. 56). Indeed, what differentiated the jury from the public was that the jury was required to assume the magistrates' ethos of impassivity. Any sign of the jury's conclusions was grounds for nullifying the trial, let alone for dismissing the offending juror. Hence the value of the partition between jury and press boxes, helping to sequester the jurors from the view of the public, and above all, the significance of obscuring the jury in shadow, so that the defense could not tailor its comments to its audience.[80] Not surprisingly, then, one of the problems in fin de siècle debates about the value of the jurisdiction of impression was to distinguish jury impassiveness from passivity.[81] In this ambiguous situation where jurors were suspended between the norms of magistrates and of oral audience, public responsiveness played a significant role in the courtroom as a substitute for jury response, while the jury itself, because of its peculiar lay status, could be counted on to respond to any imbalance in the ostensibly accusatorial proceedings.

Admissible evidence, for the jurors and the public, consisted of three sorts: the defendant's self-presentation, live witness testimony, and material objects which were piled upon a table in the center of the *barreau* just below the judge's bench. Yet if these formed the legal basis for an oral trial, this evidence, like other aspects of the trial, was nonetheless conditioned by the pretrial investigation, summed up in the dossier which loomed high on the president's desk, and which was partially familiar to the public through the newspapers. It was in light of the dossier that the entrance of the defendant was judged, while the proceedings themselves began, after the oath of the jury, with a reading of documents from the dossier. Moreover, the objects that ushers carried in to the table during the jury selection—blood-soaked clothing, knives, a vial of poisoned intestine—functioned as a sort of materialization of the textual dossier, and were so interpreted by the press, which filled the slow moments at the start of the trial with an avid inventory. Covered with traces of Troppmann's victims, this table served as a mute *partie civile*, asserting the reality of the murders to be tried with traces that embodied the absent victims. For it was across its surface that the jury watched the defendant, and the witnesses told their stories to the president, while the actual *partie civile*, if any, sat to one side of it (fig. 28).[82]

Just as the accounts of defendant and witnesses gained a moral dimension in the telling, so too was a moral life attributed to these inert objects on the courtroom table, offering another context for Walter Benjamin's observations on the 19th-century Parisian's fascination with the very imprint of human acts and implements.[83] If this process was in part a "textualization" of those objects guided by the document narrating the case against the defendant (the *acte d'accusation*), it was also a by-product of oral procedure. For the jurors' responsibility to personally scrutinize style in tandem with "content" in appraising oral testimony developed habits that carried over into the visual examination of material evidence as well. We shall see that this mode of judgment and the animation of material objects it entailed also played a part in the reception of the courthouse architecture.

Press and public paid little attention to the arrival of the judgment jury, for it coincided with the arrival of the defendant himself. Indeed, it was not until the defendant had been scrutinized that the public could attend to the swearing-in of its own proxies. Again, a jigsaw-like complexity of planning lay behind the sudden materialization of the defendant in his elevated dock. Housed, pending trial, in the newly rebuilt Conciergerie prison in the basement of the Palais, Troppmann was escorted by guards to the adjacent Dépôt de police beneath the criminal courts, and led up the spiral staircase projecting into the courtyard between the courtrooms (figs. 21, 22). From the holding room next to the stair tower (#9 on the plan in fig. 17), he could be led to the deliberation chamber for the jury selection, or down the cantilevered service passageway lining the inner wall of the courtroom (#17 in the plan) through the special door opening into the dock.

This was the choice entrance, at which jurors leaned forward and ladies and gentlemen scrambled onto their benches with opera glasses, to see whether Troppmann resembled the photographs on sale throughout Paris (fig. 23). Here was the first opportunity to compare written and printed evidence to live performance, and it gratifyingly confounded expectations. Troppmann did not look like the anticipated monster: he was small, youthful and effeminate, they found, his face even-featured and actually handsome, with an intelligent, if impassive expression, and a meek stance, with hollow chest and sloping shoulders. Jury and public saw the defendant primarily in profile, for a French defendant answered almost exclusively to the president, turning in his dock toward the bench. This inquisitorial practice created the conditions for the old tradition of physiognomic interpretation, with its interest in profile, and Troppmann was matched to those conventions. As in the contemporaneous caricatures of Victor Hugo, it was the judge whom everyone viewed full-face, while the criminal type was conceived in terms of revealing silhouette (figs. 25, 26). Hugo's image of the man of envy, the motive that would be attributed to Troppmann to explain his murders, displays the physiognomic signs that were sought in Troppmann: the "murderous" forehead and the massive jaw, with teeth that seemed, Hugo said, to watch you, just as eyes might bite.[84] Troppmann's forehead, always the crucial feature, was high and broad, suggesting intelligence, not the requisite low, sloping brow—though some illustrators adjusted it for this expectation (figs. 37, 28, 27). On the other hand, the press detected contradictory signs of bestiality—an overdeveloped jaw, with squirrel-like teeth. But most important were his outsized hands, which seemed powerful enough for single-handed murder of a group of six, and indeed were taken as such strong material evidence that a cast was made, which is still displayed in

23. Jean-Baptiste Troppmann, portrait photograph, 1869.

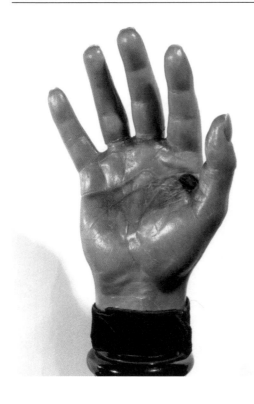

24. Cast of J.-B. Troppmann's hand, on display at the Musée de la Préfecture de police, Paris.

the museum of the Paris Préfecture de police (fig. 24). Such were the ambiguities to resolve in the proceedings: the soft, impassive face, the powerful hand.[85]

This preliminary scrutiny of the accused took place during the first step of the proceedings: the clerk's reading aloud of the prosecution's written statement of the charges, a novelistic reconstruction of crime, motive and culpability which took a full hour in Troppmann's case. Public declamation of the charges in narrative form opened the oral trial, and frankly informed the first-hand study of evidence in the courtroom.[86] In fact, the code did not provide absolute guidelines for this transition: the clerk was legally bound to read only the terse *arrêt de renvoi* giving the charges, and not the expansive *acte d'accusation*. Instead of, or just following, the *acte d'accusation*, the prosecutor had the right to present the same material orally, thus opening the debates with a personally embodied accusation. But in practice, the prosecutor remained impassive and silent, while his accusatorial text was voiced by the neutral figure of the clerk. Such a confusion of judicial and accusatorial prerogative was an accurate representation of the pretrial investigation, for we have noted that the examining magistrate who assembled the dossier and assessed the evidence was primarily responsible to the prosecutor; its roots in the rationale of magisterial disinterested authority and its uses in the courtroom are by now evident. Yet this dissimulation of

25. Victor Hugo, "Judex," caricature of a judge, drawing.

26. Victor Hugo, "L'Envieux (Barkilphedro)," caricature of a man guilty of envy, drawing, c. 1869.

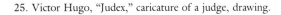

the prosecutor's voice behind the narrative had its problems: the clerk's reading was notoriously monotone, boring the jury even at the peak of its attention.

It was only after hearing the prosecution's case that the last group of participants, the witnesses, themselves part of the evidence, were normally called forward and sequestered. In reading off their names, the prosecutor provided a preview of the cast of characters, evoking murmurs of anticipation from the back of the room, but fore-closing surprises during the trial.[87] Witnesses exited through their own side door within the enclosure of benches, which led to the same cantilevered passageway that the defendant travelled to enter the dock (fig. 17). The western half of this passage constituted the witnesses' domain, reached from a spiral stair in the vestibule de Harlay reserved for witnesses (#14 on the plan in fig. 17), and giving access to a bank of witness rooms bridging the courtyard between the courtrooms (#4 and #5 on the plan). Segregated in separate rooms of unequal size, the prosecution's sixty-four wit-nesses and the defendant's five awaited the president's summons to testify. Narjoux's 1881 engraving showing these rooms supported high above the prison's exercise yards dramatizes their isolation from outside influences (fig. 22).

27. "Les tourments de J. B. Troppmann," print produced by Gangel and Didion, Metz, 1870.

The Debates

AFTER the initial confrontation of the defendant with the dossier and the withdrawal of the witnesses the oral debates (*débats*) of the trial unfolded, in three major phases: an inquisitorial interrogation, oral witness testimony, and the speeches of prosecution and defense. The ceremonial forms of these phases betray the tensions between professional and lay authority and written and oral procedure analyzed above. Moreover, they demonstrate how a lay jury and public approached their task of jointly visual and moral judgment, a practice also significant for the judgment of the courthouse architecture. Finally, the form of the debates helped shape the narratives of the crime and the thematization of Troppmann's case as it emerged during the trial. Ultimately, the interplay of judicial form and content proved inextricable from the architectural representation of criminal justice, for all three domains were addressed in terms of contested forms of authority.

The first phase of these debates was the president's interrogation of the defendant, standing in the dock—a grilling of several hours (fig. 29, which shows another

SÉANCE DE LA COUR D'ASSISES DU 28 DÉCEMBRE. — Voir page 15.

28. Troppmann during testimony on the first day of his trial, December 28, 1869, Paris.

defendant during interrogation; cf. figs. 37 and 28 showing Troppmann himself standing during subsequent testimony). While not explicitly mandated in the code, its legitimacy was upheld by the Cour de cassation; effectively it inscribed the oral proceedings to come within the deductive logic of the dossier. The president sought to expose the logical "systems" underlying the prosecutor's story versus Troppmann's, and their points of agreement but especially contestation, which the courtroom evidence would help decide.[88]

The danger was that the president would seem to impersonate the prosecutor in this unequal exchange, stirring jury sympathy for the defendant.[89] Fundamental to this impression was the difference in style between the president's and the defendant's speech, reinforcing visual differences of clothing, posture and situation in the courtroom. The president posed a sequence of leading questions, building up the elements of the case on a principle of deductive logic. That coherence was made possible by his study of the prosecutor's dossier before the trial. The defendant's responses were necessarily fragmented; he was not permitted to present a defense based on his own

29. Defendant Solleilland in the dock, Paris, 1907.

narrative structure of argument until the end of the trial. From the president's stand-point, his own questions were logical and consistent, while the defendant's attempts to respond on his own terms appeared evasive and disruptive. Consequently, the inter-rogation assumed a characteristic inquisitorial dynamic.[90]

Rather than an impartial exposition of the points of contestation on each side, the interrogation proceeded as the president's attempt to unmask the defendant, pre-sumed to be an actor concealing his true nature. Defendants were often said to resist the president's attempt to unveil their "systems" of defense, resorting instead to improvisatory surprise tactics—the shock effect of sudden refutations or new bits of evidence—well suited to the oral proceedings later on and perceived by their oppo-nents as theatrical.[91] Indeed, the defendant's best strategy was probably to fragment the magistrature's narrative of the case by casting doubt on particular points of evi-dence and logic. The agile president, for his part, devised his questions as the provoca-tion and foil for sometimes long, digressive responses, considered evasive in intent but inadvertently revealing of details of character and circumstance.[92] A standard response of the Anglo-Saxon defendant to courtroom questions—silence—was rare in the French courts, for the defendant was told that silence would be construed as acquiescence in the charges—a judgment that should be considered in the context of French self-ascribed volubility as well as that of the jury's job to study the performance of the defendant.[93] The defendant, like the other evidence in the trial, was forced to be eloquent.

In Troppmann's case, President Thévenin's strategy was to discredit any evidence Troppmann might present as competition to the narrative of the prosecutor. The ideal response from the defendant was acquiescence with remorse, conforming to the scenario of self-discipline developed in the Enlightenment *drame bourgeois*. But even confessions could take challenging forms. Between his arrest and the trial, Troppmann had made three different confessions, each claiming a different role for himself. In the second statement, Troppmann accepted sole responsibility for all the murders; in the third, he retracted, claiming he had had accomplices whom he dared not name, but to whose identity he offered clues which the magistrature had not pursued. The *acte d'accusation* had explained Troppmann's inconsistency as moral evidence of bad character and guilt; it presented the crime as a melodrama in which the virtue of the Kinck family, who had achieved wealth by honest work, was eclipsed by the evil and jealous Troppmann, who sought to usurp its wealth, and in which the final act would be the reinstatement of the forces of good by the court. In questioning Troppmann, the president was obliged to engage Troppmann's claim of accomplices. Troppmann confronted him: Why won't you follow up my clues? The president's answer: How can you expect us to take your clues seriously when you lie habitually? By repeatedly reading out inconsistent passages from the confessions and forcing him to state that he had lied, the president definitively discredited the defendant's words. Thus the key point of contention became whether Troppmann was physically capable of murdering several children simultaneously—for only in that case could the prosecution dismiss the question of accomplices. This was an issue that jurors could appraise through visual scrutiny of the defendant. Yet even here, Troppmann's verbal inconsistency was read into his demeanor; his mild demeanor was expected to be deceptive, for in duplicity would inhere the consistency of his character.[94]

The next phase of the trial, the witness testimony, was less inquisitorial in character, for witnesses stood at the bar in the center of the *barreau* and spoke spontaneously (figs. 30, 31). But like the defendant, they testified directly to the president, considered more impartial than defense counsel or prosecutor, although in practice he prompted the intimidated witness with leading questions.[95] Isolated at the bar, their backs to the public—unlike their American counterparts—the witnesses' stance and gesture were crucial, honing the public's skills at the kind of interpretation that the critic Edmond Duranty would advocate, just a few years later, for Impressionist art: "A back should reveal temperament, age and social position, a pair of hands should express the magistrate or the merchant, and a gesture, a whole string of feelings."[96] Indeed, artists for the popular press developed, in the 1880s, a substitute for the

30. Testimony in the trial of Trochu, Vitu and Villemessant, held in the southern pendant to the criminal courtroom, Paris, 1872 (after the Commune fire had destroyed its decoration).

traditional views of trial activity set within the courtroom: a genre of pages of composite vignettes to convey the characters of the multiple actors in a trial, fulfilling Duranty's program in the mass media, and matching and encouraging a skill already extant among the public.[97]

Implicit in the rationale for oral witness testimony was the question of moral evidence: the jury's job to consider the credibility of the witnesses as well as the character of the defendant. Since witnesses were often character witnesses, this was especially significant. The defendant had the right to comment on each testimony, as well as the right, shared with the prosecution, the defense lawyer and the jurors, to question the witness. Related to this procedure was the deliberate staging of confrontations between witnesses and between witness and defendant, intended to provoke candid, revealing emotion, as shown in a court artist's vignette from the Panama trial of 1893 (held in the larger new courtroom of the first chamber of the Cour d'appel) (fig. 32).[98]

Confrontations in Troppmann's trial were, above all, moral confrontations bolstering the story of vice versus virtue, as portrayed in a popular print commemorating

31. Vignettes of witnesses testifying in the trial of Senator Humbert against *Le Matin*, Paris, 1908; jurors' bench at upper left.

the affair (fig. 27). Quantities of witnesses testified to Troppmann's solitary, brooding nature, his single-minded preoccupation with an audacious scheme to bring wealth to his family, and the intellectual prowess suggested by his fondness for reading and his skill in chemistry; they also testified to the virtuous, uncomplicated character of the Kinck family, united in fond obedience to Kinck *père* (see the vignette at the left in fig. 27). Indeed, the foreignness of the Alsatian witnesses, largely German-speaking, led the Parisian *Petit journal* to characterize them as simple-minded and naive, constituting by extension, a "moral photograph" of the Kinck family's simple-mindedness,

32. Confrontation, as seen from the jury box, in the Panama trial, held in the new Première Chambre of the Cour d'appel, Paris, 1893.

contrasting with the predatory intelligence of their obviously deviant compatriot Troppmann. As the *Petit journal* further pointed out, the cumulative effect of the witnesses was to keep courtroom attention focused on the absent victims—indeed, it went so far as to observe that the trial opened "providentially" on the anniversary of the massacre of the innocents, reconciling mythic and historical calendars.[99] But the most dramatic confrontations were those embodied in the person and deeds of the witnesses themselves, and for this the prosecution turned to an episode in Troppmann's arrest at Le Havre, when Troppmann had slipped away from a gendarme and tried to drown himself in the harbor. Hauguel, the young boat-caulker who saved Troppmann for trial and had been decorated for bravery, made a sensation in the courtroom as an epitome of young French manliness, the counter-type to Troppmann. Reporters described his military bearing, so unlike Troppmann's; the president addressed him a formal thanks, actually provoking an unrepressed round of cheers and applause from the public. Hauguel fixed the theme of brave heroism versus cowardly murder, offering a meaning for Troppmann's disconcerting androgyny.[100]

Despite the comforting explanations of melodrama, however, Troppmann troubled his judges. The press marvelled continuously at Troppmann's imperturbability in the face of confrontation. Far from betraying his feelings, Troppmann's comments mainly verified his intellectual sangfroid. Why should Troppmann's impassiveness have been worrisome, when even he acknowledged that he had murdered? At stake was legibility and explanatory power. Jurors were responsible not simply for assessing factual evidence, but for persuading themselves that they could imagine Troppmann committing the murders. That obliged them to square Troppmann's appearance with an act requiring Herculean vigor and agility—as Troppmann himself pointed out.[101] Moreover, the jurors did not merely decide whether Troppmann committed the crimes; they also determined whether he could be held responsible for them, and to what degree.[102] If he could describe the murders without expressing feeling or remorse, did he comprehend the gravity of his acts, and could he be assimilated to the prevailing moral or psychological system?[103] Was he insane—grounds for acquittal? Indeed, for the president and for reporters, Troppmann's impassivity was an antisocial act, a piece of incriminating evidence, as remaining silent would be: by thwarting the desire to interpret signs, it became meaningful in itself.

There was one category of witnesses that directly addressed this crisis in legibility: the experts who offered assessments of moral and material evidence considered not reachable by layman's inspection, and who gained an increasing role in criminal trials during the course of the century. In Troppmann's case, there were three: two medical doctors and a chemistry professor. Although appointed by the president on the rationale that they were to give a disinterested professional assessment independent of the interests of either side, at Troppmann's trial they were classed as the final witnesses for the prosecution. The doctors Bergeron and Tardieu, both familiar and celebrated figures in the criminal courtroom, concluded on the basis of examination of the bodies of the victims and defendant that Troppmann could have murdered three children at once: while his constitution appeared "frail [*débile*]," his "nervous energy" and his profession as mechanic had developed in him "great agility and flexibility [*souplesse*]," "in the wrists especially, an above-normal strength," with "great precision," which equipped him for simultaneous stranglings. The chemist confirmed Troppmann's surprising ability to fabricate the poison that killed Kinck *père*, as embodied in the (ominously) Prussian blue color of the remains in the test tube on the table piled with material evidence.[104] The danger with experts, however, was that they would report with so much professional authority that the jurors would take umbrage at that challenge to their own ability to judge the evidence.[105] Ultimately, it fell to the prosecutor and the defense lawyer to offer in their speeches internally consistent narrative explanations of the ambiguities, and indeed of the relatively disordered mass of testimony.

The speeches, the final phase of the debates, formed an entirely different genre from the previous debates: models of rhetoric and stamina delivered over the course of hours. They called on the oratorical skills that were mainly developed in the context of civil cases, where well-placed classical erudition might impress and entertain the judges and where brilliant legal reasoning was of the essence. But the speeches in the criminal courts were different in so far as they were calculated to appeal to the lower middle-class juror and made sense of live, as well as recorded, evidence, selectively discounting and highlighting its elements in competing accounts of cause and effect, motive and responsibility.

Commensurate with the asymmetry of the courtroom, the standards for argumentation for and against the defendant were markedly different, to the point that the speeches carried different names: the prosecutor's *réquisitoire* versus the defense counsel's *plaidoirie*. Justice Nouguier declared in his professional manual of 1868 that the prosecutor must exercise voluntary self-restraint, precisely because he represents the weight of the social order against an individual defendant.[106] As the spokesman for the social interest, the prosecutor enjoyed immense powers. But in post-Revolutionary French justice, it was by law and temperance, rather than by deployment of superior force, that society justified its right to punish. In his *Discipline and Punish*, Foucault has pointed out the shift in political economy from the ancien régime's display of deliberately excessive force to repress the violence of individual challenges to order, to the post-Revolutionary polity's insistence on the display of measure and legal restraint to replace the evident violence of punishment. What is striking here is how French jurists justified the retention of the powerful prosecutor within an ostensibly accusatorial procedure and ideology, through the model of that exemplary self-restraint that the defendant allegedly lacked. Self-restraint was to be expressed not only by tone but by emphasis on the general abstract principles that were understood to underlie the codes and render them not merely a list of laws, but a universal guide for self-conduct. The prosecutor was to emulate the abstraction and anonymity of that written law, carrying it into oral procedure. Justice Nouguier wrote of the prosecutor's *réquisitoire*:

> I applaud him if his words faithfully represent his convictions, because justice has no *parti-pris*, if they are humane because he serves human justice, moderate because justice knows no hate, calm because justice lacks anger,

male because justice is a virile power in an organized state, austere because each word echoes morality and law.[107]

The defendant's lawyer, however, represents an individual in contest with a vast social body: to redress that balance, he must become his client, speaking for him better than the defendant could do himself, expressing his case with all the dramatic resources he could conjure. He must move his audience emotionally, by exposing the failures of the social order under the principles evoked by his colleague from the point of view of the particular history of an individual, challenging the prosecutor's abstractions through feeling and specificity, and even provoking him to step out of role into an imprudent response.[108] Said Nouguier,

> At his disposal . . . is every mode . . . reason and logic, laughter or tears, movement and fireworks. If he dazzles, a ray of his bright eloquence may illuminate the one he defends. When, by irony and sarcasm, he arouses laughter, the judge may be moved to say, with the poet, 'I have laughed, here I am, disarmed.' If he fascinates his listeners, excites their pity, perhaps he will move the jury to acquittal through emotion, where reason would have failed.[109]

Nouguier's prescriptions represent, however, a formal defense of French judicial practice against an initiative of the Second Empire government. For the government had attempted since at least 1860 to restrain the defense by compelling lawyers, through disciplinary action, to adopt more deferential demeanor and speech towards the prosecutor in the courtroom. That initiative seems only to have increased resistance among defense lawyers, of whom Troppmann's lawyer Lachaud was among the most theatrical.[110]

Theatrical excess was legitimate for the lawyer, the self-employed professional, while it was not for the magistrate, who was a civil servant. That difference was evident not merely in the rhetorical style of wording, but equally in the gesture and use of the space of the courtroom that modifies speech and makes it plausible to its audience. This was obvious to the courtroom artist Morel who drew up the courtroom vignettes for the Eyraud and Bompard affair of 1890 for the popular journal, *Le Monde illustré* (fig. 33). The prosecutor stood at his desk on the judges' tribune, to give his speech; as the artist indicated in the sketch at the upper left, his plausibility depended on merely raising a finger to emphasize a point. But the defense counsel, confined to his bench by a high barrier designed to hold his papers, was compelled to use gesture to bridge the vast *barreau* between himself and the jury. Pacing within his bench, he would embrace the table of evidence in gesticulation, lean intimately towards the jury, point back to his client, exploiting the dramatic silhouette enabled by his full sleeves, as seen in the sketch at the lower left.[111]

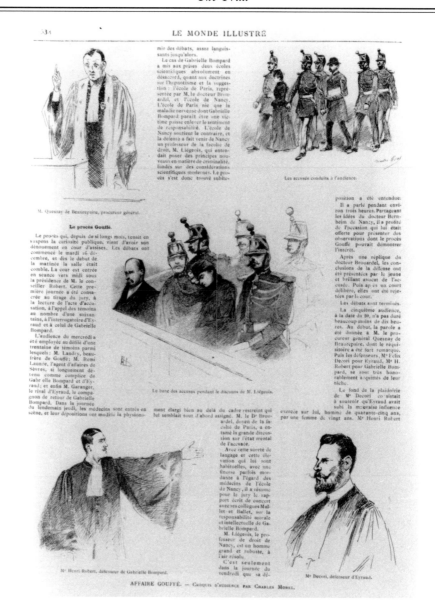

33. Vignettes showing the prosecutor (upper left) versus the defense lawyer (lower left) giving their speeches in the trial of Eyraud and Bompard, Paris, 1890.

Costume played a significant role in the complicated job of the lawyer, whose success depended on his skill in playing the role of another individual, his client, while persuading the jury that his words expressed his personal *intime conviction*. Precisely because the lawyer spoke for someone else (and was so often likened to an actor), it was essential that he develop a style that would be recognized as his alone, and which would represent his personal stake in the case he had chosen to take on.[112] Now his robe and *toque* constituted a uniform, which concealed the individuality of the wearer's body and assimilated him to a professional ethos. But in so doing it showcased the most expressive body parts, face and hands, essential to rhetoric. These gestural and expressive aspects of pleading actually gained importance in the post-Revolutionary courts, as lawyers ceased to read prepared texts and strove for at least the semblance of an oral, improvised performance.[113] And during the 19th century, the individuality of the lawyer's style, attested in the press which made his reputation and codified into galleries of verbal portraits in contemporary books on famous lawyers, came to permeate his very robe, hitherto a means to efface individuality. Contemporaries commented on the differences with which lawyers and even magistrates wore their robes and *toques*, interpreting them as marks of personality:

> There are differences in the quality of robes and in the ways of wearing them: most often the hem is raised, but sometimes it drags . . . *Toques* also . . . take different forms under the impress of the thumb of their owners. . . . Magistrates no longer constitute a fixed type; they are as variable as humanity itself. Sometimes you will see emerge from his courtroom door a tousled judge, *toque* over ear, robe dishevelled, other times the figure of pomposity or of elegance.[114]

Personality could be read in the way the robe hung and creased and developed spots of wear. The 19th-century commonplace that successful lawyers wore their robes threadbare implies more than lawyers' display of their special disdain for wealth and fees, which helped sustain their moral credibility as more-than-professionals;[115] more subtly, it was a means to mark that uniform to the utmost with the imprint of the individual wearer. Not only did the robe simplify, condense, and dramatize such revealing gestures as the tilt or hunch of the shoulders and the sweep of the pointing arm, the robe itself deformed in response to the wearer's most habitual gestures. Thus the skills of interpretation and judgment that we observed at work upon the objects on the *table à conviction* and upon the person and performance of witnesses, were equally exercised upon and encouraged by the lawyer. While the prosecutor resisted that phenomenon with impassiveness in order to uphold the transparent discourse of universal law, the lawyer drew on costume and performance—indeed theatricality—as a means to persuade his audience of his sincerity in the service of the individual.

The *Petit journal* introduced its readers to the Procureur général Grandperret, at Troppmann's trial, in terms that popularized and personalized Nouguier's generic prescription for a prosecutor: "His aspect is a bit severe perhaps, but isn't that appropriate to a man who represents the whole of Society?"[116] In his nearly three-hour speech, Grandperret presented his job as one of throwing impartial light on a criminal who sought refuge in shadows, and told the jury its job was to force Troppmann to take responsibility for his acts. In a worn metaphor which regained force from the literalness of its fulfillment in the side-lit courtroom, he declared:

> He has used every artifice to sustain, in the evidence, a few shadows in which he can hide; but an avenging light has attached itself to him, permits him no repose, and shows him to us, inexorably chained to his victims.

For obvious reasons, the prosecutor grounded that avenging light and emotion in Troppmann and disengaged his own words of enlightenment, which were couched in the language of universal reason and led to an appeal to judge not by emotion but by obedience to "eternal justice." Focusing on the ways Troppmann had duped his victims, he warned the jury not to be duped itself by a criminal who "knew how to compose his features." His major addition to the *acte d'accusation* was to elaborate on Troppmann's manipulation of the family's unshakable trust in father Kinck. Grand-perret argued that Troppmann's inconsistent confessions matched his ambiguous, deceptive appearance, and enjoined the jury to trust in magisterial and expert author-ity to unmask Troppmann's audacious crime against "eternal justice," whose victims exemplified the virtues of the patriarchal, law-abiding family. Its emotive content thus neutralized, Grandperret's story was this: The prosperity of the Kinck family, built on work and thrift, should have inspired the impoverished but able Troppmann; instead, ambitious Troppmann, filled with dreams of inventions rather than patience for labor, eliminated the entire family to seize its earnings (see fig. 27, vignette at bottom). Worse yet was Troppmann's method, exploiting filial piety and wifely devotion to patriarchal authority to lure the wife and children to their deaths in Paris. Tropp-mann's demand that the police look for accomplices was merely another trick to gain time, and perhaps an escape. Troppmann's chafing at authority, his will to turn his wits to profit, was his undoing.[117]

As customary, the defendant's lawyer spoke second. For Lachaud, gifted in oral improvisation, this was an opportunity to shape his defense as a response and as an alternate bid for the confidence of the jury. Speaking to a courtroom whose hostility to Troppmann had peaked under Grandperret's sway, Lachaud amplified the scale of the vengeful forces ranged against his isolated client and insisted that justice de-manded examination of defendant as well as victims. Contrasting his own indepen-dent status to Grandperret's, he also distanced himself from the discredited Tropp-mann, telling the jury that he was giving them his personal conviction as a judge of Troppmann, like themselves. This line of argument quelled hostile reaction from the public and even won a few signs of approbation.[118]

Specifically, Lachaud argued that it was unconscionable for the prosecutor to condemn Troppmann on the basis of Troppmann's own words; one must step outside

Troppmann's statements for an independent appraisal of all the evidence, a juror's task for which Lachaud conducted a demonstration. Returning to the central question of whether Troppmann murdered alone, Lachaud argued that a layman's critical analysis of the courtroom evidence proved he could not—especially the model of the field at Pantin (fig. 28). But the jury judged as a court of last resort, it could not mandate an additional investigation of Troppmann's clues to accomplices, and Lachaud knew the issue was only good for shaking the jury's confidence in Troppmann's responsibility.

The question of responsibility thus took precedence over proofs of accomplices. Lachaud argued that, far from willful defiance, Troppmann could not help his crimes or his lies. Lachaud was famous for throwing the moral responsibility of an acknowledged criminal into question, and for stimulating interest in the defendant through his courtroom effects.[119] Capitalizing on thwarted desire, he pointed to Troppmann and declared: "You want emotion? I will show you emotion. All I need do is mention Troppmann's mother!" At which Troppmann, for the first time, collapsed in tears in the dock[120]—illustrating Lachaud's case that Troppmann was not an unequivocal enemy of family, but rather a deranged boy so possessed by the desire to rescue his own impoverished, cheated family from its disasters that he could stop at nothing. The misfortunes of Troppmann's inventor-father forced the young man to desperate, paranoiac tactics. Confronting Troppmann's lack of remorse over the murders to his tears for his mother, Lachaud declared Troppmann a monomaniac, a 19th-century category of madman possessed by a singular idée fixe which governed his reasoning and acts and perverted his feeling. In Lachaud's hands, emotion and its absence were legible symptoms of insanity, grounds for lenience from the jury.

It is striking that both speeches, drawing on such different sources of authority, thematized authority itself, and did so in terms of the family, an institution that bridged the particular case of Troppmann and the social order at large. According to Lachaud, Troppmann's idée fixe was his perverse filial piety; according to Grandperret, it was insubordinate ambition—a telling characterization, for monomania was first defined in the early 19th century as a disease of excessive ambition in the absence of ancien régime sources of authority. Indeed, as of 1869, ambition and authority were what remained of that once-popular construct, for psychiatrists themselves had discredited its medical value during the 1850s and even Lachaud's charisma proved inadequate to revive it.[121] Thus Grandperret was able to magnify the case into social allegory: Troppmann had attacked the foundations of social order, a hierarchy grounded in the family and which was understood to culminate in the patriarchal emperor himself. In Grandperret's terms, working class ambition had but two outlets, Troppmann's path of subversion, or Jean Kinck's path of obedience. The difference was explained in gendered terms. Whereas Kinck achieved success by masculine self-control and participation in the social order, Troppmann refused his example, substituting less-than-manly passion and wiles. Building on the reporters' perception of Troppmann's appearance, even Lachaud stamped Troppmann as feminine, by asserting his jointly immature and pathological inability to control his feelings.

Gendered authority was equally at stake in Grandperret and Lachaud's competition for the jury's confidence. Grandperret's speech was masculine and severe in style and demands, asserting the necessity for self-control and moral accountability; from a later perspective, his emphasis on self-control was equally a call to the often insubordinate institution of the jury to internalize magisterial norms and authority. Lachaud's speech was emotive and theatrical in style and counselled lenience, asserting the power of sentiment, not only in the deranged Troppmann, but also for the jury, which was supposed to judge by its own impressions.[122]

The final phase of the trial formed a web of formal replies, in which Troppmann waived his right to the last word. But it was President Thévenin who actually had the last word, for after closing the debates he presented his own hour-long résumé, supposed to be an impartial summary of the partisan arguments by the two sides, which would clarify the issues for the jury and purge them of distorting passion. An institution so tainted by accusations of unfairness that it was abolished a decade later, the résumé was on this occasion received by journalists as "impartial and lucid."[123] It was the prologue to the list of questions which the President then put to the jury, addressing seventeen counts of murder, theft and forgery, and adding to the charges in the *acte d'accusation*.

The jury was out for forty-five minutes, while a restive public noisily anticipated the outcome, and Troppmann himself waited in the defendants' holding room. Jurors' judgments were in principle inviolably private or *intime*, throwing each man upon his individual conscience. Disagreement among the jurors during deliberation was concealed by a rule of utmost secrecy; no juror was to reveal what had been said or the balance of the voting after the fact, nor was he necessarily to know how individual colleagues had voted. Following merely optional debate, but significantly with access to the inquisitorial dossier (minus the witness depositions) and to advice from the president, the jury decided by majority vote whether Troppmann was guilty of each count and whether there were extenuating circumstances. Jurors filled out secret ballots at individual desks with sequestering barriers set at each place around the jury's table, and deposited them in the symbolically important urn, whence the foreman drew and counted them. At 9:30 p.m., a bell alerted the public and judges to the jury's return, and the foreman stood, "very pale and violently agitated," to read the verdict to the bench: guilty on all counts.[124] Accepting the judgment, the president called for Troppmann, who was brought to the courtroom to hear the verdict from the impersonal, that is, corporate, lips of the clerk.[125]

Verdicts typically came at night, when artificial light played on the darkened courtroom, coloring it with the fatigue and anticipation of all participants (fig. 34):

34. Reading of the verdict, Eyraud and Bompard trial, Paris, 1890.

At that moment in time, the courtroom presented a lugubrious aspect. Only the bench was lit, by three lamps whose shades projected the lamplight downward, leaving the upper part of the room in shadow; the gas jets of the two chandeliers had lost much of their brilliance and cast only a faint glow. The gold highlights of the ceiling turned to red; the oak panelling black-

59

ened. . . . The public was enveloped in shadow; the candles of the court stenographer were extinguished. Troppmann, standing in the dock, seemed to float in a twilight zone.[126]

The assistant prosecutor then proposed the death penalty mandated by the code for assassination; the judges retired momentarily, perhaps to debate the sole option permitted them by the code—to make the execution private—before returning to sentence Troppmann to the public guillotine. This was the moment of completion, for the judges' words were sovereign. Applause erupted from the audience, which was hushed by ushers while Troppmann was led from the courtroom.[127]

THE HISTORY
OF THE RIGHT
TO PUNISH

THE ARGUMENT that won a guilty verdict was probably that Troppmann's crime was a daring yet cowardly attack on the very patriarchal model that could have saved him from distress—a form of parricide, dangerously close to regicide.[128] In looking back on the trial, anti-imperial Third Republic commentators viewed the proceedings and their outcome as a didactic, spectacular reassertion of political authority at a decisive moment of challenge to the Empire, a regime fatally based in the emperor's personal patriarchal authority. It was said that the Empire had made a scapegoat of Troppmann, whose crimes were so heinous that the government had little difficulty rallying the public and jurors against him and deflecting attention from the problems of the regime itself.[129] Troppmann's twilight came to be seen as the twilight of the Empire.

Yet at the time of Troppmann's execution, the death penalty was somewhat sparingly used and the object of republican protest.[130] For one thing, this spectacle called up the specter of Revolutionary terror and ancien régime torture at a time of unrest, when the crowd might rally against the government's organized violence to a courageous convict.[131] For another, it belied the conviction that France was ever advancing from a primitive barbarism—epitomized by the ancien régime's secret criminal trials and deliberately bloody public punishments—to more perfect civilization, in which justice was humane and supple. In his speech, Lachaud himself had pointed out that a proposal for abolition had just been discussed in the Sénat, and that a more modest proposal to sequester executions from the public eye was pending; however, he acknowledged a contemporary view that, however much public opinion abhorred the death penalty, France had not yet reached a stage of civilization that could do without its value as a deterrent. Nonetheless, he invoked the jury's power to override a law out of phase with social mores, compensating for the slow, conservative legislature.[132]

In fact, the practice of French justice had evolved towards greater lenience since its establishment under Napoléon, through the agency of the jury. The codes had proved so severe that juries often acquitted, alarming authorities who dared not simply abolish the jury. The solution was the law of 1832 which not only softened the codes of penalties but also allowed the jury to award extenuating circumstances, obliging judges to reduce the penalty. Extenuating circumstances outpaced acquittals as the agent of equity, of lenience, of social adjustment of the code to the special circumstances of the individual.[133]

The very notion that the jury could exercise equity, invoked by Lachaud and enhanced by the law of 1832, returns us to the question of the basis of justice, or the locus of sovereignty. One's views on sovereignty informed one's opinion about who held the right to punish, and indeed, to what degree this power was a right. For the constituency that lodged sovereignty in the sacred person of a monarch, or for those who sidestepped that option to lodge sovereignty in the disembodied text of the codes, justice was a matter of universal and timeless values which stemmed from or replaced religious authority in ethics. For the Second Empire judge Lambert, the president's job was to inculcate the sacred values of the code in his jurors, and by extension, in the public.[134] The right to punish lay in the codes or in the magistrates who served them, and the jury must be helped to internalize their values. Yet for those who believed that justice stemmed from the populace and its values, the codes lacked such suprahuman transcendence; they remained documents authored by individuals in particular historical circumstances. This was not to discount their authority entirely, but rather to justify the idea that those written documents required ratification and even updating by the living public based on changing social conditions and commensurate values. The legislature, officially responsible for updating the codes, was not adequate to this task on its own because it dealt with law at a general level, not the level of its application to particular cases. Those who linked jury service to voting rights were prone to argue that the jury functioned in a complementary but limited fashion to update the codes in practice, bringing them into phase with evolving mores. Such a historicist, relativist concept of social values had fostered the law of 1832 and gained increasing acceptance in the rapidly changing France of the latter 19th century.[135] For those who adhered loyally to the codes, acquittal or extenuating circumstances in cases in which juries believed the law inappropriate for the individual offense were outrageous—instances of a lay jury claiming "omnipotence," placing its sovereignty above the law. Yet it was the code itself that charged the jury with determining whether a defendant not only performed a given crime, but was guilty of it; moreover, the code empowered the jury to decide on the basis of its moral convictions as to guilt, even when these conflicted with courtroom evidence. The controversial aspects of the jury system were intrinsic to the Napoleonic codes and were merely acknowledged by the law of 1832. The compromise written into the codes had laid the conditions for a historically evolving dispute over the locus and nature of the right to punish.

That dispute demonstrates that the problem was not merely a matter of who held the right to punish, but of how the juror construed the responsibility of the defendant and the purpose of punishment. In the courtroom, as we have seen, the prosecutor and the lawyer laid this problem directly before the jurors by seeking to sway them respectively in favor of code or equity. As several historians have recently demonstrated, jury equity was justified by revised conceptions of criminal responsibility, challenging the old idea of individual free will with the idea that individuals are constrained by physical and social circumstances such that they are not uniformly liable for their actions. From the early 19th-century premise that uniform enforcement of the code would best guarantee equal justice, France moved towards the practice, established in the Third Republic, of calculating punishment not in terms of the crime, but the psychology and circumstances of the individual criminal.[136] It was not only the inquisitorial powers held by magistrates but the practice of discretionary judgment deployed by jurors that brought what Foucault called modern disciplinary power into the courtroom.

That historical development was counterbalanced by a change in emphasis from the interests of the individual to those of society, for which the Second Empire was probably the watershed. Judicial discourse, both mainstream and opposition, from the 1820s to the Second Empire, emphasized the individual, whether through the question of individual free will, or the reform of an individual convict, isolated in a cellular prison so that he would be forced to reflect on his conscience, or the reinforcement of the rights of the defendant, whose social circumstances came to command special consideration. Initially, new attention to the social circumstances of the defendant fostered periodic verdicts of extenuating circumstances—such that jury practice sometimes matched the kind of judgment that Victor Hugo demanded in 1862 for his celebrated Jean Valjean of *Les Misérables* (a novel whose claim that a poor man could be sentenced to forced labor for stealing bread stirred debate in the press).[137] But ultimately the idea of making exceptions to the code became a standard practice, exercised as much in the interests of the social order as of the defendant.

Especially in the wake of the Commune, judicial discourse assumed a new emphasis on social order and interdependence juxtaposed to the dangers of assemblies and crowds, the latter epitomized for conservative politicians and a significant public by the Communards. The practice of "individualizing" judgment not only gained new justifications and currency,[138] but it also exacerbated the crisis of legibility or the basis for judging, evident in the Troppmann trial, by recasting the old lay grounds for judging in terms of the new expertise of the human sciences, particularly criminology. The reallocation of judgment of character from the lay jury to expert witnesses in psychiatry or criminology, advocated by such reformers as Cruppi, was informed by the articulation of a systematic attack on the crowd (*la foule*), a category in which the courtroom audience and the jury itself were included. For jurists like Cruppi and Gabriel Tarde, the corrective and alternative to those unreliable live publics was renewed participation in a reading public, or expert knowledge, because these activities required individual isolation and reflection and forestalled the theatrical dynamics of live events.[139] Indeed, by the early 20th century, the Ministry of Justice was to marginalize dramatically the Parisian criminal courts with their juries. Not only did it shift further numbers of criminal cases to the jury-less misdemeanors courts, but it built the latter a spacious new wing at the Palais, itself lush and protective in architectural character but less popular in its system of judgment.[140]

The Second Empire constituted an interlude in this transition, in which the government turned against the focus on the individual. Government judicial policy was newly repressive, asserting uniform criminal responsibility through the free will doctrine and devising new means to influence the magistrature, although the habits and image of juried justice tended stubbornly towards lenience. To solve that problem the government reduced the case load of the criminal courts so drastically that Paris no longer needed the two criminal courtrooms the administration was building in grand form. By legalizing for the first time the practice of downgrading certain crimes for trial by the non-juried misdemeanors courts, the Empire made the criminal courts more of a showcase for a restricted category of sensational cases. However, the last, defensive years of the Empire saw the lifting of some restrictions on political activity and a rekindling of reform debate, including judicial reform, creating an ambiguous political climate for the inauguration of the criminal courts and for Troppmann's trial. Under the liberal ministry of Ollivier, announced on the eve of Troppmann's trial, the character appropriate to French criminal justice, the showcase of the modern judicial system, was again open to question.[141]

The contest of the individual versus authority (itself generalized and abstracted as "society") at the core of the criminal trial was articulated in terms colored by gender and class, a discourse that was also extended to the building and its decor. In the Second Empire, self-control and lawfulness were increasingly associated with masculine intellectual capacity, rather than with human nature, and were thus deemed uncommon among women and the restive working class.[142] While Troppmann's lawyer lost the case he based on partial insanity, irresponsibility for uncontrollable impulses was a common plea, especially associated with a trend towards female crime which drew much attention in the Third Republic. Madame Clovis Hugues, for instance, used the west vestibule of the Palais to shoot a man who had falsely accused her of promiscuity, and was acquitted in the criminal courtroom (fig. 35). Such acquittals were received with mixed emotions: while they attested to the jury's assimilation of updated theories about the inherent weakness of groups such as women, they were also said to evidence the jury's own irresponsible sentimentality.

The association of equity with feminine susceptibility to emotion probably explains a complaint made by trial reporters about the character of the new criminal courtroom. Too rich, especially in gold, it was like the elegant female audience that crowded spectacular trials such as that of Madame Hugues, and which compromised, said contemporaries, the masculine duty of repression (fig. 36). In this interpretation, visual appeal to the senses invited theatrical behavior, which signified and encouraged challenge to social authority—a challenge most apt to come from women and the lower classes, who were prone to respectively elegant or gaudy display. Indeed at Troppmann's trial, women had been relegated to the back of the room.[143] By contrast to the feminized atmosphere of the jurisdiction of impression, a popular illustrator of

35. Madame Clovis Hugues shooting her adversary in the west vestibule, Paris Palais, 1884.

the Troppmann trial unconsciously substituted the stern neoclassical courtroom evocative of male severity, graphically expressing the major criticism the new wing aroused at the trial and at its inauguration (fig. 37; cf. fig. 28).

In effect, the restraint expected of magistrates and jurors resembled a sumptuary law: because magistrates held such a wealth of power, they should display it only

36. Vignettes from the trial of Madame Clovis Hugues, Paris, 1885.

sparingly, especially in contrast to the defense, whose style is abundant, rich in self-expression, theatrical in address, precisely in order to claim power. The self-controlled style of the magistrature exemplified the ethos deemed necessary to self-government in lieu of absolute monarchy; it drew its persuasive power partly from the negation of theatrical display formerly associated with the monarchy and now increasingly transferred to "women" and the "crowd" in the courtroom, those sectors with the least actual control over the material resources that had supported royal display. Historically, this austere style had required the reconstruction of traditional visual signs of authority which were particularly important to architecture, especially the representation of wealth and sex. While wealth remained an attribute of authority, explicit material display was reascribed from the ruling class to the least privileged; simultaneously, gender remained a sign of authority, but its characteristics were also inverted, such that masculinity was redefined not in terms of royal splendor but of middle-class self-restraint.[144] This rationale associating ethics with aesthetic modes was equally applied to the architecture of the courtroom. What the print of Troppmann in a neoclassical courtroom invoked was the image of the courtroom developed in the late 18th century and standardized in the early 19th century, when many new courthouses

37. "Jugement et condamnation de Troppmann," print produced by the Imagerie Pellerin, Epinal, 1870.

were built in the provinces specifically for the new judicial system consolidated by Napoléon. The neoclassical courthouse focused the image of modern justice in the first half of the 19th century, with its portico and its often apsidal courtrooms, their ceilings relatively plain and their walls sometimes architecturally framed by pilasters and soberly decorated, favoring sculpture and—significantly—inscriptions over representational painting.[145] These basilican settings set the stage for a veneration of the written codes and their unbending application, then the prevailing professional doctrine of judicial practice.

It is significant that the old criminal courtroom that Duc was replacing in the Paris Palais did not date from that period (fig. 57). Installed in a Gothic wing of the Palais which stood just east of the new criminal courtrooms and was slated for reconstruction as part of the appellate courts, it was remembered as a shabby, plain room, dark and low-ceilinged, with one prestigious if dilapidated remnant from its pre-Revolutionary life as a courtroom of Parlement: an allegorical fresco covering its coved ceiling.[146] While respected enough that the administration attempted to salvage it before demolishing the old courtroom, Bon Boullogne's late 17th-century ceiling painting, an illusionistic, proto-rococo allegory of Justice repressing crime and ensuring peace, abundance and an exemplary flourishing of the arts, was hardly in keeping stylistically or representationally with the austere image of justice of the day; nor was the courtroom as a whole equal to the expectations of reporters such as Timothée Trimm (the pseudonym of Léo Lespes), who declared:

> For the application of the ultimate severities of the law, to condemn a defendant to death, it seemed to this writer that the courtroom was inadequate. By its meanness it undercut the majesty of that terrible decree. Public opinion seemed to demand for the exercise of that greatest right of legal repression an imposing, monumental local, in harmony with the terrible role of those called to represent the Defense of Society and Obedience to the Laws.[147]

Trimm's expectations for the new courtroom—a newly monumental austerity suitable to a code of law and its strict enforcement—were widespread, as was the association of severe style with masculinity. Duc's decorated courtroom challenged that standing assumption that criminal justice was austere and masculine and aroused a debate about the representation of justice which associated class and gender with the tension between accusatorial and inquisitorial aspects of the criminal trial. The debate was complicated by the fact that public commentators such as Trimm demonstrated a divided sympathy for the two modes. It was not uncommon for reporters, members of the courtroom public that responded theatrically to the agonistic trial, to condemn that response after the fact, blaming not only the respondents but also the stage that seemed to have provoked their own lapse from a normative code of self-control. If Troppmann and his courtroom stood convicted in 1869, the verdict was, as we have seen, not entirely confident.[148] The tensions in the practice of judgment offer insight into contemporary dilemmas, not only over social ethics but also over how ethical modes should or could be associated with aesthetic forms. The reporters' reaction to the courtroom extended the critical discussion of these issues that had begun a year earlier.

The Inauguration of the Criminal Wing and its Critical Reception

T HE INAUGURATION of the new wing in October 1868 raised the problem of judicial character but in specifically architectural terms.[149] As one critic pointed out, it was an exceptional inauguration: in lieu of ceremonies, the government held a week-long open house, opening even the back stage dependencies, inviting comment.[150] Reviews were varied, suggesting no official interpretation—indeed they puzzle precisely over interpretation. Thus the event provoked an intriguing interpolation of official intention and decorum at the period when restoration of a legislative voice was at issue for the Empire.[151] The response of the critics raised two interrelated issues: not only the thematic and prescriptive question of what the architectural character of justice should be, but also the basis for judging character in architecture. Authority, represented above all through images of class and gender, was the central problem here: whether the courthouse belonged to the partisans of orality or textuality in the trial, whether it was to be judged on the basis of oral or textual habits, and whether, in fact, the public commentators were willing to stake positions on either side of this attested divide.

Critics most often discussed the courtroom as an integral part of the new building, in which it culminated a processional sequence that they traced from facade to vestibule to courtrooms. The facade was not yet visible from the street; to see even the exterior of the new wing was a special event. To attend the open house, you presented yourself at 17, quai de l'Horloge, that is, on the north quay at the northwestern corner of the Palais (still a construction site for the additions to the Cour de cassation), just east of the place Dauphine. The street between the Palais and the place Dauphine, the rue de Harlay, was closed by gates at the time, for the 17th-century houses lining both sides were still in use before their impending demolition; they sheltered the Prefecture of Police while its new quarters were under construction at the south side of the criminal wing. The new criminal wing loomed out from within a *pâté* of decaying and rising structures. Only in 1875, after the row houses had been razed to create a forecourt and to open the entire west facade to views from across the Seine, was its monumental staircase completed and put into public use.[152] That future prospect was widely illustrated in the press at the time of the inauguration, when only the entrance facade of the criminal wing, together with its sculpture, was finished. Thus inspection of the wing started with the facade, necessarily scrutinized at close range, a vantage point also illustrated in the press by an engraving based on a photograph in the architects' archives (fig. 38; cf. fig. 6).[153]

For art critics, the facade offered an even more important character than the courtroom, for it served as the physiognomy of the institution. Its character too

38. Photograph of the west facade at time of the inauguration in October 1868, photographer unknown.

provoked controversy. Commentators of all sorts debated: was it severe or elegant? This question centered on the architect Louis Duc's choice of classical order—his handling of the column together with its base and entablature, whose elements and proportions were governed by norms. The conventional bearer of meaning, the order demanded particular attention in this facade—because of its giant dimensions and scale, because although these columns were engaged, or integral to the wall of the facade, their depth lent them the corporal presence of freestanding columns in a portico, and because they structured the facade into huge open bays, whose porousness itself signalled and invited public entrance.

Yet in inviting scrutiny, the order defied categorization on the canonical scale from the masculine Doric, stocky and strong, to the matronly Ionic and the maidenly Corinthian, increasingly slender and elegant—shown in the three central orders in the didactic comparative chart from Vignola's standard treatise, represented here in a 19th-century French edition (fig. 39).[154] Precedent dictated either the Doric for severity or the Corinthian for majesty. While most labelled the facade's order an idiosyncratic, severe form of Corinthian, one critic reported it as Doric, and others noted that it combined features from the Doric and the Corinthian—for instance in the entablature, which fused Doric triglyphs and metopes with Corinthian proportions and actually transformed masculine triglyphs into female-headed consoles.[155] Equally ambiguous were the capitals, considered the column's physiognomy and thus the face of the building in miniature: these combined chaste Doric shape with budding Corinthian foliage, confounding genders in an image of adolescent androgyny—ambiguous like Troppmann's gender, but resolved from the polarized male and female capitals that Duc had used to represent alternately force and justice in the facade of his earlier wing for the misdemeanors courtrooms at the Palais (figs. 41, 42).[156] The allegorical bas–reliefs on the low panels plugging the intercolumniations explicated the hybrid aspect of justice, polarizing it into pairs of forceful versus protective qualities whose identities were didactically published in the contemporary press (fig. 40).[157] Yet this representational sculpture maintained the ideal tradition of all-female allegories, whereas the architecture surprisingly realized and embodied the hybrid in an anthropomorphic gendered image in which masculine austerity and severity dominated for most critics.

The point is not that the facade was "about" gender, but rather that it appeared to employ the symbolic language of gender, with its powerful political implications, as a means to characterize modern justice in the terms in which it was popularly and professionally discussed—those of textual severity and of popular equity. Certainly gender would have remained merely a latent reference in its orders, had the architect not made a liaison between genders. But in the event, the order yielded by that liaison was for many the most expressive and the most mysterious aspect of the facade. The power of gendered imagery was moreover intensified by the implication of the human body in these combinations of architectural elements, at once corporal and fragmented.

An additional factor in response to this facade was its broken entablature, interrupted by females (figs. 38, 41). Grangedor declared that this destroyed the serenity of the horizontal line of the cornice, trivializing the facade into a work of elegance rather than severity.[158] But Charles Blanc praised the eloquence with which the sculptural activity of the facade resolved into a grave horizontal, and declared that the columns

LES CINQ ORDRES D'ARCHITECTURE D'APRÈS BAROZZIO DE VIGNOLE. PL. I.

TOSCAN.   DORIQUE.   IONIQUE.   CORINTHIEN.   COMPOSITE.

39. Comparative chart of the orders from a French edition of Vignola's *Regola delli cinque ordini d'architettura* [orig. 1562]: P. Eudes, *Vignole* (Paris, 1836).

and female-headed consoles were robust because they were more than an ideal image of classical order: they were doing actual work, buttressing the vestibule vaults, signalled by the voluminous roof and the arched openings of the facade. In this argument, Blanc was conducting a lesson in what he termed "architectural eloquence," demonstrating how this facade made evident to a viewer the complex relationship between exterior and interior sometimes only apparent in the analytical drawing of a cross-section (fig. 21). For not only did the orders declaim the ideal order of the codes, which jurists have long called the "édifice juridique," but they enabled and denoted an actual voluminous space where the live public would pursue its judicial interests.[159] Here was another ambiguity, which Blanc approved: what was ideal and perfect as against what was specific and contingent on real circumstances.[160]

40. Engraving showing the six relief figures in the west facade (including fig. 4), based on photographs by Richebourg, n.d.

The polarity of ideal versus contingent was couched in terms of architectural types, such as one could see in the old east facade, where buildings of different historical periods stood cheek by jowl—particularly the ideal neoclassical portico in the courtyard, image of uncompromising order, versus the adjacent arches and barrel vaults to the right, which signify the old French Renaissance waiting hall directly inside, with a richer, more flexible character (fig. 5). Based on a search through the architect's papers and drawings just after his death in 1879, the architect and critic Sédille pointed out that Duc had entertained alternative types in a series of studies for the west facade and vestibule, including a festive arcuated French Renaissance hall and the severe colonnaded basilica (figs. 43, 44). Ultimately he fused these types in a facade of rich severity which came to him, Sédille said, through the image of the

but he dropped the distinctively Egyptian cavetto
cornice which appears in the 1852 drawing (fig 44).

41. Detail of the capital and entablature, west facade.

bastardized, yet primordial temple of Denderah in Egypt—an object of contemporary fascination, whose reproduction in a print Duc may have clipped from a book review in the *Revue générale de l'architecture* (fig. 45).[161] The vestibule extended this hybridization, fusing the two-storied interior of the basilica, the subject of 19th-century studies and reconstructions, with the French vaulted waiting hall (figs. 46, 48). Outside and inside, in the rhetoric of mural articulation as in spatial distribution and configuration, Sédille, like Blanc, discerned a drama between a transcendent ideal order and the arcuated space of active change, quoting a rare disquisition by Duc himself on this theme.[162]

While the order dominated the facade, the arch and vault literally created the spacious vestibule. Sédille suggests that Duc transformed this fact into symbolic terms, contrasting the ideal unbending force of the order, whose plastic form occupies and commands space like an orator, to the flexible arch and vault, whose imbricated

42. Detail of the male- and female-headed capitals, second floor level of the facade of the wing originally built for the Tribunal de Police correctionnelle, Palais de Justice, Paris, Duc and Dommey, completed c. 1852.

forms energetically configured the voluminous interiors necessary to post-Revolutionary public activity. The vault traditional in the French Renaissance waiting hall not only provided a more obviously capacious alternative to the open-truss or flat ceiling of the ancient basilican type, but created the opportunity for a didactic juxtaposition between order and arcuation—in which these idiosyncratically flexed vaults became emblematic of that feminine quality of equity.

Appropriately, the colossal order that articulates the walls of this vestibule is Ionic, a feminine companion to the masculinized, forceful order outside (figs. 48, 20). But again, a peculiar order, with a hypertrophied face, half console for the vaults, half capital for the order, as though the vaults and the order were not of the same species and had to be reconciled by will (fig. 49).[163] Moreover, the vigorous sculptural force of that head dissipates into the wall, to which it transmits the thrust of the vaults; below, the body of the pilaster deflates to a thin plane, reemerging only in a sculptural foot. Where its counterpart on the facade commands space for itself, this order is deferential, framing space for the live public to occupy.

Yet no critic felt the need to belabor the well-established role of the orders in imparting a modular discipline to interior space, particularly an interior so porous, so much the permeable vestibule, as this one. These pilasters extended the open framework of the facade to the interior, whose long east wall opens up at either end into the great east-west corridors traversing the Palais, bracketing the open screen behind which the pair of stairs gave public access to the two elevated courtrooms. (Even here, however, visitors sensed the specificity of their access to justice, thanks to the array of private doorways labelled for specialized participants, such as witnesses, in the wall below the stairs.) But simultaneously, this colossal order rationalizes the relationship

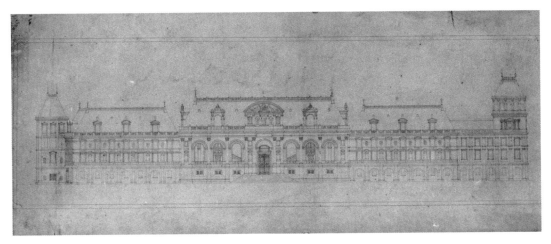

43. Duc and Dommey, project for the west elevation of the Palais, drawing, c. 1847.

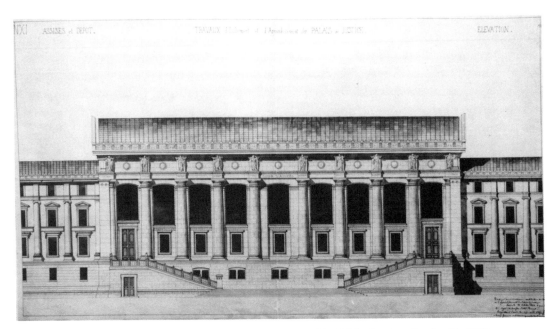

44. Duc and Dommey, intermediate project for the west elevation of the Palais, drawing, October 21, 1852.

45. Temple of Denderah, Egypt, elevation, print by A. Titeux, in H. Horeau, *Panorama d'Egypte* (Paris, 1841), as reproduced in the *Revue générale de l'architecture*, 1847–48.

of the elevated courtrooms to the double-height vestibule it spans. For the vestibule uses two additional orders to simulate a two-story basilica. Its lower level is demarcated by a Doric frieze, surmounted by a balustrade which is figured in relief on three walls but becomes actual on the east wall where it lines the courtroom stairs and landings. The upper level, framed by an order matching the chaste Corinthian of the facade, emulates the upper gallery of a basilica, here partly virtual, partly actual. However, the colossal Ionic pilasters that unite Doric basement and Corinthian gallery and support the vaults infuse the vestibule itself with Ionic character. At the entrance to the courtroom stairs, the standing sculpture by Duret confirms the association of the Ionic vestibule with Law, a partner to the Force of the facade, leaving the rich upper story of the courtrooms to Perraud's seated Justice with her urn (Justice *assise* for the Cour d'assises), in the Corinthian aedicule crowning the Ionic entrance (figs. 52, 20).

Again, vantage point helped condition interpretations of this architecture. Most importantly, the physical experience of climbing the courtroom stairs fosters close-hand scrutiny of this complex and suggestive detailing, including the little columns duplicating the order of the facade. Like Troppmann's impassive face in the courtroom, to which his judges tried to impute a psychology, these exacting profiles were studied by critics, who acknowledged Duc's obsession with telling shape, stressing his conscientiousness and their indubitable signification even where they could not read his meaning (figs. 50, 51).[164]

What was unmistakable in this climb to the courtrooms, however, was its culmination in richness. If those severe Corinthian capitals proved ambiguous, the detail-

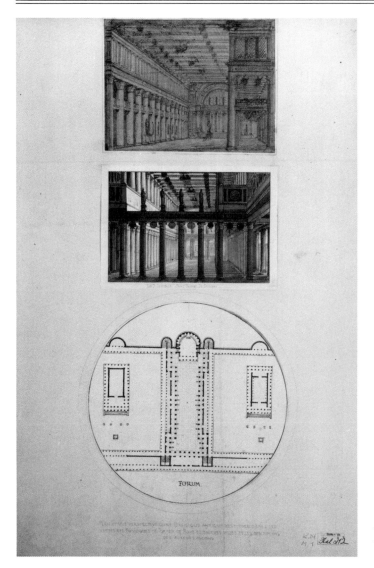

46. J.-I. Hittorff, reconstruction of an ancient basilica, drawing, 1831.

ing of the vault consoles for the landings at the top of the stairs, forming the lobbies for the courtrooms, is Composite, the most ornate and festive on the canonical scale (fig. 39). Not only richer detail but polychrome marble intarsia makes a transition from the monochrome walls and vaults of the vestibule to the colored atmosphere of the courtroom (fig. 53). From Force one progressed to civilizing Law, and finally to the efflorescence of Justice in practice in the courtroom.

Open-house visitors arrived in the courtroom through the public doors, as a member of the public would later enter a trial, though they then toured all its zones,

47. Photograph of the northernmost of the two large east-west corridors (the galerie des prisonniers), looking west.

48. Photograph of the west vestibule, looking south.

49. Photograph of a capital/console in the west vestibule.

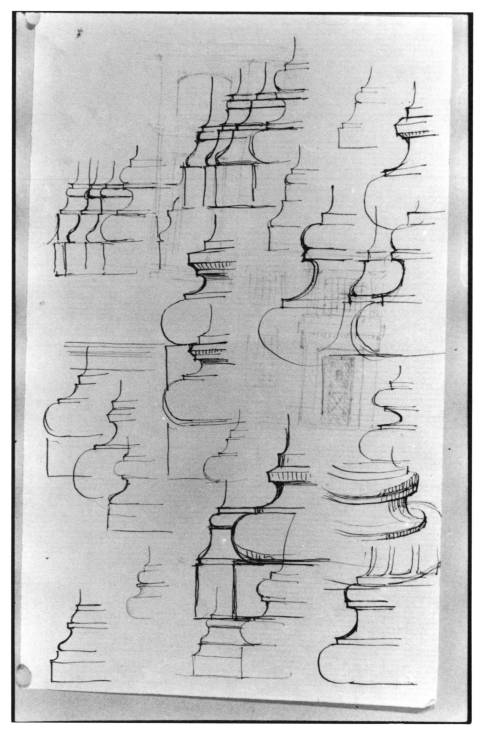

50. Duc, sketches for the bases of the colonnettes in the criminal courtroom stairs.

51. Photograph of a colonnette base in the criminal courtroom stairs.

52. Lampué, photograph of the entrance to the stairs leading to the criminal courtroom, showing Perraud's seated Justice in the aedicule above and Duret's statue of Law in the niche below (the placement of Duret's Law was modified in the 1960s).

53. Lobby of the criminal courtroom, at the top of the stairs from the west vestibule.

even the back stairs leading down to the prison. Thus, they first experienced the courtroom from the public end, gauging its long, narrow shape along its lengthiest axis, and inspecting it in the unilateral sunlight from the clerestory windows puncturing one side wall. Whereas they had entered the long, narrow vestibule broadside, their first experience of the similarly-shaped courtroom emphasized the hierarchical potential of this volumetric type, organized like a gallery-less basilican church in a progression from narthex (standing room area) to nave (benches), to chancel (that restricted area of the *barreau* framed by the bench, the dock, and the jury box).

54. Criminal courtroom in its current state, looking east towards the judges' bench.

Reviewers perceived the room in relation to its social purpose, using their imaginations to situate future trial participants within it; likewise, illustrations of the courtroom accompanying reviews in the popular press depicted the room in generic use (fig. 56).[165] That experience of the room as a socially-zoned interior, in which individuals occupying different roles were spatially located, was reinforced by the plethora of private entrances, and was additionally shaped by the decoration.

The courtroom today still presents a golden ambiance, with its warm oak panelling and the gilded highlights in the coffered ceiling, but has been stripped of some of its original decoration (figs. 54, 55). We can reconstruct the critics' experience by combining the current state with the original decoration of the room shown in the first illustrations cited above (fig. 56). Sumptuous by contrast to the vestibule, whose monochrome masonry struck Grangedor as unduly cold, the courtroom embraced the public in a warmly colored environment, which nonetheless displayed an internal decorative hierarchy which helped to create the hierarchical sequence of zones described earlier.[166] Coordinated by the architect, the decoration was graded from simple wall panelling and ceiling coffering in the areas for public and witnesses, to the richer

55. Criminal courtroom in its current state, looking west towards the public entrance.

zone of the *barreau*, where the ceiling breaks into compartments for representational painting, to the judges' tribune, against a rear wall with high panelling and additional paintings.[167] In the panelling alone, orthodox Corinthian pilasters in the public zone give way to Composite ones in proximity to the magistrates. However, the paintings—which included the first mural paintings to be commissioned for the Palais during the renovation campaign then in progress for thirty-three years—were what most obviously distinguished this courtroom from others in the Palais, and from the sculptural realm of the facade and vestibule.

It was the richly coffered ceiling that most impressed viewers, with its allegorical paintings by Léon Bonnat. These drew their program, as a journalist pointed out of the counterparts in the south courtroom, from Prud'hon's *Divine Justice and Vengeance Pursuing Crime*, painted in 1808 specifically for the old criminal courtroom though long since removed to the Louvre (figs. 58, 59).[168] But where Prud'hon made his figures of Vice and of (Assassinated) Virtue both male, Bonnat explicitly gender-typed the figures in his central panel.[169] His Justice represses a male Crime and protects a female Innocence. Like the public, architect and artist both ascribed gender to the acts

LA NOUVELLE SALLE DE LA COUR D'ASSISES DE LA SEINE; dessin de MM. Bertrand et Jules Pelcoq. — Voir page 742.

56. Criminal courtroom at the time of its inauguration, print.

of force and justice, which were also more conventionally figured in a pair of grisaille niches on the wall above the judges. In keeping with the Corinthian-Composite courtroom, Bonnat's Justice is herself a gentler soul than Prud'hon's. She has no need of Vengeance with her torch, for she radiates light, like the bas-relief of Truth in the facade (fig. 40, second from left; fig. 6)—reaffirming that persistent theme of the light that reveals the telling detail.[170]

The representation of justice through images of gender and splendor—in this case explicit light symbolism rendered as a dazzling brilliance—provoked more controversy; the anxiety of this debate drew energy from that larger ambivalence about whether authority should be displayed with splendor or dissimulated with a self-disciplined and severe austerity. Not only in Bonnat's painting but throughout the courtroom, critics recognized the dominant theme of light imagery, previously noted in the unilateral window-lighting, the situation of defendant and jury, and the imagery of the prosecutor's speech. They acknowledged the pattern of gold highlights in the decor, focused in the crucifixion by Richomme which hung above the president, a standard fixture of courtrooms but unusual in its gold ground which caught the light from the windows.[171] Rather than spiritualizing the room, critics said the gold made it worldly and luxurious, insouciant of the misery of the defendant. They insisted upon material, sensuous associations, which they linked to theatrical femininity, rejecting Bonnat's contrast of virtuous feminine grace to masculine bestiality. And they questioned Bonnat's style together with his symbolism, for his vigorous, plastically modelled figures seemed to elbow their way into the real space of the courtroom, eschewing the abstraction of allegory and of the flat architectural plane to which they belonged.[172] This decor begged that pervasive courtroom question of the character, not merely of transgression, but of authority.[173]

Those doubts testify to the instability of the visual signs and social values at stake. Clearly critics condemned as inappropriate what they construed as theatrical visual display—what I have called a revival of iconicity. It is less clear what kind of justice or, indeed, whose justice they thought this decor represented. Was it a representation of themselves as a theatrical public which they rejected, or a representation of the Second

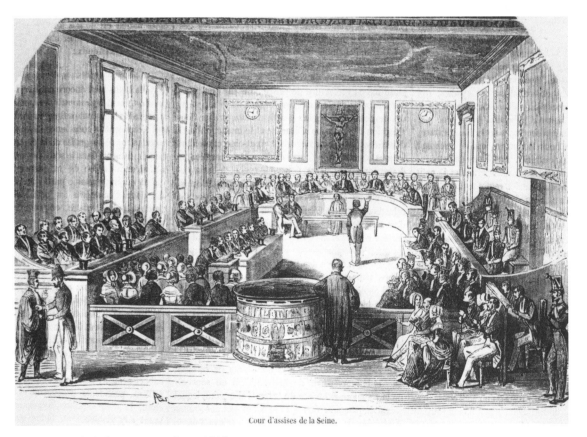

Cour d'assises de la Seine.

57. Previous criminal courtroom, print, c. 1846.

58. Prud'hon, *La Justice et la vengeance divine poursuivant le crime*, 1804–08, painted for the first criminal courtroom, now at the Musée du Louvre, Paris.

probably —

Empire government as anachronistically self-indulgent? Is their response a parallel to the trial reporters' censureship of the volatile courtroom public, suggesting the capitulation of public spokesmen to the anti-theatrical values represented by the magistrature? The example of Charles Blanc indicates that critical response was not uniformly associated with obviously conservative social arguments; other critics also voiced concern that the public and press gain good vantage points for overseeing trials, and that the jury be accomodated so as to enhance its independence and importance in the proceedings. Yet granting some diversity and independence in the political stances of the critics makes their general concensus on the courtroom (unlike the facade and vestibule) all the more striking. For if such was public reaction, what possessed the government to present a courtroom that was effectively perceived as representing

96

values inappropriate to social authority? The imperial government put its name on the new wing and on the courtroom in particular, through the Napoleonic eagles and initials repeated in its wall-hangings, and most explicitly through the portrait-bust of Louis-Napoléon mounted above the dock. Yet to accept the room as a representation of Second Empire justice still left ambiguity, insofar as Louis-Napoléon presented himself as the successor to his uncle, founder of the Napoleonic codes and modern judicial system assimilated to the neoclassical courtroom type.[174] If the imperial government was reconstructing the textual aspect of modern justice in iconic terms, it had reinforced repressive authority in the courtroom. At that moment, was the iconic courtroom to be understood as autocratic and regal or as insurrectional and popular—or in terms of both excesses?

The Third Republic government's sensitivity to the critics' complaint was evident in how it handled repairs immediately after the fires set in the Palais by the Communards in 1871. Recommissioning most of the decoration in this courtroom, it eschewed the gold-ground crucifixion, giving the job instead to Bonnat, who produced

59. Bonnat, central ceiling painting, criminal courtroom, orig. 1866–68, destroyed 1871, recommissioned 1872.

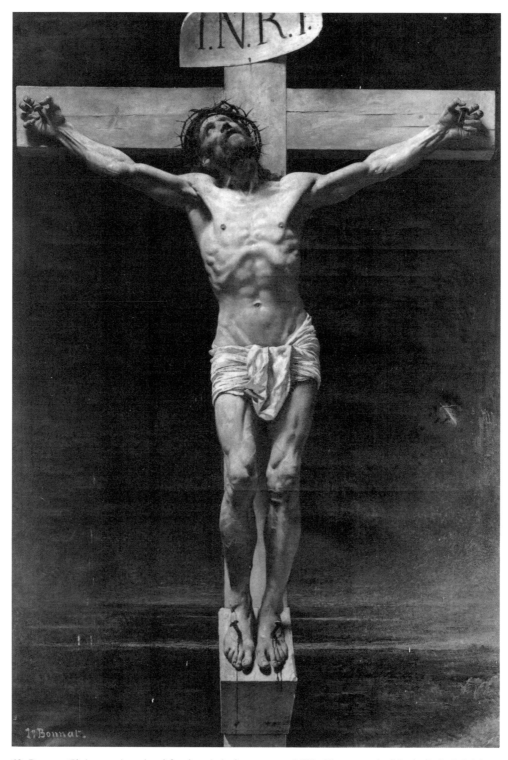

60. Bonnat, *Christ en croix*, painted for the criminal courtroom, 1872–74, now at the Musée du Petit Palais, Paris.

an image that provoked renewed controversy (fig. 60). Critics described how Bonnat erected a cross in a remote courtyard of the Ecole des beaux-arts, affixed a cadaver to it, and painted his *nature morte* as it decomposed. So sculptural, so material was Bonnat's depiction of stress and pain that critics complained he had painted the criminal, and not the body of the lord—an image evocative of the Third Republic courtroom intent upon the psychology of the criminal.[175]

But the government did not repudiate the overall richness of the courtroom. The official rejoinder to the criticism of feminine richness appeared *within* the critical debate. Blanc, partially sympathetic to the project, pointed out that Duc had resurrected the French Renaissance type for the courtroom, with its sculpted, gilded ceiling, epitomized by the former chamber of Parlement, whose decor Duc persuaded the government to allow him to restore in a historical reconstruction based on a print of the 1787 *lit de justice* (fig. 1).[176] Acknowledging that its rich form originally housed a severe phase of French justice, Blanc proposed that Duc was reviving the rich type to give it its proper significance, that of civilized modern justice:

> What sort of character should our modern courthouses have? Should it be terrible, severe? That is one's first response, based on our idea of justice, still bound up in our minds with the idea of punishment and still darkened by the now-distant, though persistent, memory of the torturer-executioner. Yet on reflection, one recognizes that an image of ferocity no longer suits modern justice, and suits future justice even less. Before the Revolution, the parlements exercised terrible cruelty. Despite the protests of Montaigne and the philosophers, they sometimes ordered—even in civil cases—torture *des coins*, torture by the boot, torture by lead melted into the ears, and other inventions borrowed from brigands. I have read in the *Journal de Barbier* . . . that a young man who stole a watch from a doctor in a courtroom was judged on the spot, condemned to death and hanged within the hour. For a monument in which judges made such decisions, no architecture . . . could be savage enough. Even the temple of Paestum would hardly suffice, with its squat supports, formidable architraves, rude triglyphs, and the narrowness of its column spacings and the violence of its profiles. Well, who would have thought it! Those parlements were sumptuously lodged. They wanted the courthouse to rival the royal residence in magnificence. Here I speak not only of the historic Palais de Justice of Paris, which was long inhabited by the monarchy. . . . but of the other parlements of the monarchy, such as the splendid ones at Rouen and Rennes. The Palais of the Parlement of Normandy was an architectural marvel. That of Rennes boasted exceptional splendor, with beautifully worked panelling, and ceilings with coffering which was sculpted and gilded, whose compartments

were painted by Jouvenet. Its judges were lodged and furnished like princes of justice.

It is by recalling those traditions that Monsieur Duc arrived at the character he would give to the new palace of the law. He told himself that in modern civilization, justice must present itself in the mind, not as a menace but as a protection; that this Palais built for the future must bear witness to the more humane sentiments to which we have come through the progress of philosophy and the softening of social customs; that if we permitted ourselves such pomp in former courtrooms, all the more reason today to temper by elegance the majesty expected of the "building of our laws," as the magistrature calls it. This was the point of departure for Monsieur Duc. . . . [In the courtrooms themselves, Duc] revived the amplitude, the comfort and the magnificence that the architect associated with the old parlements, based on the idea that he had formulated of modern justice.[177]

In so arguing, Blanc, who appears to have discussed the matter with the architect, proposed that Duc's idea of modern justice was the gentle and civilized one of a man known to have subscribed to a Saint-Simonian doctrine of the progress of civilization.[178] To temper majesty by elegance, in the name of a more understanding type of justice, was to replace the icon of the king, who once embodied justice (however much the *parlementaires* disputed his authority), with an equally spectacular performance, an apparent sharing of authority in the modern juried court associated with protections for, even lenience towards, the defendant. Duc's revival of the decor associated with the traditional seat of the *lit de justice* under the ancien régime should be linked to Bérard's observation that "nowadays, the *lits de justice* are held by public opinion."[179] Yet Blanc himself had reservations about this sort of character for a criminal courtroom, and declared that its richness, if intended as a sign of equity, could equally be interpreted as a materialist display of class-based power over the defendant:

I confess that I myself have some difficulty with a criminal courtroom so grandiosely decorated. I conjure up a poor man, in the grip of poverty, having been stupefied by ignorance, who is brought there in worker's clothing [*en blouse*] to account for a theft or a murder, under those gilded ceilings, vermilioned and illustrated with splendid paintings. What will that poor man think of a society that spends so much money to condemn him and so little to instruct him. . . . Yet my job is to consider the issue of art, and I will not grudge praise to an artist who has revived with such knowledge and taste, the traditions of magnificence that he believed to be appropriate.[180]

Blanc questioned the implications of richness here in a way that appropriately recalls the comment of the major architectural critic César Daly at the inauguration, some thirty years before, of Duc's youthful monument to the July Revolution which still stands on the site of the Bastille. Musing on the triumphant aspect of Duc's Composite column, Daly had wondered whether it was possible to reconcile the aspect of mourning for the July victims buried in the crypt with the celebration of the revolution.[181] Duc's courtroom seemed to Blanc to celebrate the triumph of society rather than to mourn the loss of a citizen. As Foucault among others has pointed out, an impoverished murderer's very readiness to die, for the sake of a voice in court and in the press, a sort of immortality, destabilizes the society that tries him.[182] Perhaps it was because that dynamic was recognized by the administration and the judiciary that Duc's criminal courtroom did not mourn the defendant but instead addressed and aggrandized the juror and by extension society. This, in any case, was the argument advanced, in response to critics like Blanc, in the quasi-official account of the building published in 1881 by Félix Narjoux.

In an interpretation based on contact with the architects and reviewed by Paris administrators, Narjoux presented a professional, judicial rationale for reviving the old French Renaissance type: that majesty was necessary to inspire awe and obedience from defendants and jurors alike:

> The courtrooms are very rich—some have said too rich, because they have not taken into account the impression that these rooms must make not only on the mind of the accused . . . , but also on that of the jurors . . . It is indisputable that a man is influenced by the milieu in which he is placed, and when a man sits in the dock or in the jury box, it is necessary that the architecture move him. In a nondescript courtroom, cold and mean, the architecture cannot help the juror to comprehend the gravity of his role, the weight of the terrible responsibility that he assumes. In a room in which the forms, proportions and decoration are out of the ordinary, able to astonish and surprise, his emotions are different, he feels that he has been removed from his milieu to an exceptional, abnormal situation. As for the accused, hardened as he may be, can he help being involuntarily impressed, if not moved, by the grandeur surrounding him, the radiance which strikes and astonishes him? He finds himself suddenly transported from his dark cell to a room filled with splendor; the paintings, the gold shimmer before his eyes; he feels all eyes fixed on himself; he watches the slow arrival of the magistrates who will decide his fate, one at a time, rustling their long robes; he sees them take their place at an elevated bench, virtually a throne, before a respectful, attentive crowd; he may then compare his miserable state to the situation he could have acquired or maintained, and often, perhaps, a vague aspiration will rise in his heart and lead him back to goodness. For such a mise-en-scène, which cannot escape a certain theatricality, what is needed is something out of the ordinary, the use of violent means, and one of these

means was the creation of splendid, richly decorated courtrooms, augmenting the prestige of the social order in the name of which the courts will strike the defendant brought before them.[183]

In Narjoux's proto-Durkheimian account, the rich ambiance of the courtroom inspires the desire to fuse with the society that the courtroom represents, and so unites the diverse constituencies in the courtroom in social solidarity, and indeed, a common polity. That such "theatricality" could equally generate the reverse response—active disputation and difference—was a risk or paradox that France had encountered before. As Mona Ozouf has pointed out, the men of the Revolution had felt it necessary to organize live festivals to animate and make compelling the textual basis of the Republic, even though the tradition of the festival harbored the threat of spontaneous resistance to or inversion of authority.[184] More specifically, those men of reason had organized the festivals to appeal to the senses of the populace, only to experience the unravelling of the Rousseauian premise that natural concord existed between Enlightenment reason and the senses. The criminal trial, especially in the new courtroom, constitutes a historical sequel to this problem of the festival, as it was integrated into the practice and physical form of a definitive social institution.[185]

In this essay, I have looked at the criminal courts from the point of view of contemporaneous trial-participants and critics. What emerges is a debate about who the courtroom belonged to: the defendant *en blouse*, the juror and the public, or the magistrate. We have seen how much hung on their verdict. Different constituencies— including the art critics, who appraised the wing in terms of its expression of purpose—came to disparate conclusions about whose justice was rendered there, and, consequently, how their parts in a trial could best be played. Such conclusions about the physical and moral character of the architectural "person" of the criminal courts concern the life of the building in use. In concentrating on what might be called the ritual significance of the building, they attempted to interpret the intention of the government agencies, magistrates and architects who funded, designed and executed it. We have already seen the effects of this interpretive effort: the courtroom specifically gathered new meanings, and was altered in relation to interpretations of its intended meaning, during the first years of its life in use.

Since I have focused on the reception rather than the production of the criminal courts, I have not yet addressed the possibility raised by Blanc and Bérard, and disputed by Narjoux and Lenormant: that the courts belonged above all to their architect. An architect in Duc's position enjoyed considerable freedom, but was most restricted in dealing with precisely the issue of richness, especially as it literally represented public expenditure. Yet a story recounted by Bérard about the inauguration indicates that Duc's rich courtroom did not please the magistrate who oversaw the

criminal courts, the Premier Président of the appellate courts, Adrien-Marie Devienne. Bérard recalled twenty-five years later:

> When it emerged from the hands of the workers . . . , the courtroom was
> swimming in gold, gilt dominated the somber tones, and everything glit-
> tered; the architect, in presenting the courtroom for the first time to the
> First President of the court, M. Devienne, awaited his reaction eagerly; but
> the latter said coldly, in that distinguished and subtle manner in which M.
> Devienne was wont to utter profound things: "With such a courtroom, it
> will be necessary to dress the defendants in silks."[186]

Was this rich character then Duc's alone—an idea that the adminstration later felt
compelled or persuaded to endorse? Although we know that contemporaries placed
great stock in architectural legibility—witness Blanc's review of Duc's criminal
courts—and that the administration devoted substantial resources to representational
public architecture, we know all too little about how character and iconographic
programs were conceived. The architect, particularly one with Duc's prestige, already
established by his July Column when he was appointed to the Palais, expected
to exercise artistic discretion. He was supposed to conceive a decorative program
to enhance his architecture, he proposed and oversaw painters and sculptors notwithstanding their own prestige, and he generally worked out the related architectural detailing of his project after it had passed the national and Parisian adminis-
trations' architectural review boards, when it was no longer subject to collegial
interference.

On the other hand, the host of review committees to which the architect
answered—architectural, artistic, political, financial, and, in Duc's case, judicial—
carried significant power and commented, sometimes antagonistically and definitively,
on matters of character. While Duc may hold prime responsibility for introducing a
new iconic image of criminal justice, he cannot be dissociated from the judicial milieu
in which he had worked for nearly twenty-five years and which did take a role in his
work. And to the extent that this initiative may have been Duc's, it was a representation of justice that, as I have demonstrated elsewhere, he had only developed through
a slow and painstaking interaction with the historic Palais and the place of history in
the identities claimed by the modern courts. If support was lacking in President
Devienne, it appears to have been whole-hearted in Devienne's predecessor, Claude-
Alphonse Delangle, who was deeply involved in the definitive phase of planning the
criminal courts wing both as a magistrate and as Prefect Haussmann's ally on the city
council, and who endorsed the notion that courthouse architecture should impress
and instruct through splendor. Indeed, the Parisian administration, including its con-
scientious review board for decorative programs, accepted Duc's project and escala-

tion of richness, in the face of demands for greater severity and austerity from the more traditional architectural review board at the national level.[187]

To ask the traditional question about attribution (whose courthouse is this?) as a way to fix meaning is problematic, as Jacques Derrida has pointed out.[188] The more useful point is the problematization or thematization of judgment that the architecture, like the trial, seemed to entail. The architecture of the criminal courts was peculiar, indeed sphinx-like, in that it appeared meaningful and yet defied easy access. Its very ambiguity and its deliberate juxtapositions of different orders and types raised problems of legibility and authority evident in the trial. It provoked the viewer to interpret the exacting details for him- or herself, and thus replicated in the response to architecture the problem of inferring psychology from the material evidence of the body. In this process, inanimate architecture was reanimated, fetishized, as it revived theatrical visual imagery or iconicity within the social conditions of a new political economy epitomized by self-restraint.[189] In specifically representational terms, the debate about criminal justice and its basis of authority took form in visualizable qualities, particularly class and gender; Duc gave them visual form, which was assimilated into a continuing negotiation of what French justice was or should be. As we have seen, this architecture, viewed as part of a debate over representations of criminal justice, belongs to a social phenomenon involving a shift in emphasis from code to procedure and courtroom trials, and from text-conditioned imagery to a new form of iconic imagery. Commentators were sensitive to the theatrical appeal of the architecture, and its atmospheric aspect, which Narjoux described as a self-conscious construction of mood through architecture, a manifestation of the environmental influence on behavior which intensely interested the Third Republic. Indeed that self-consciousness underlies even Cruppi's critique of the architecture, in his attempt to return criminal justice to a text-dominated procedure and imagery that would nonetheless retain the aspect of equity which critics like Blanc attributed to the rich courtroom.

We have looked at the iconicity of the criminal courts wing in terms of the social history of justice, as a departure from the established image of Napoleonic justice in the neoclassical courthouse, its order associated with a universal code and its strict enforcement. The neoclassical courthouse had functioned as a part of the iconography of text-based authority, rather than procedural flexibility. On the other hand, its very consistency made for a kind of iconicity, even if its ultimate subject was displaced from the ruler to the rule, the written law. In breaking apart and reconfiguring that model, the criminal courts building necessarily sacrificed iconographic clarity and stability. This was probably deliberate on Duc's part, in order to establish a more historically specific yet evocative representation of justice. What was at stake here, according to Blanc, was the matter of architectural eloquence, or perhaps more accurately, architectural reception. Duc was hardly the only architect to be pondering these problems.

If one looks at Duc's criminal courts in terms of architectural history and intention, it is likely that Duc was responding to another alternative to neoclassicism, represented by the Bibliothèque Sainte-Geneviève, completed in Paris in 1851 by his colleague and friend, Henri Labrouste. Neil Levine has argued that Labrouste's building portended a decisive break with the presentational, iconic mode of the classical tradition by elaborating a new mode of architecture based on the act of reading. Eschewing the orders or any sculptural relief that might imply bodily form, Labrouste gave his building hard, smooth surfaces of clearly inanimate stone in which he inscribed his idea of the library in meaningful signs, passages available to be read only in disjunct segments, like the pages of a book, and assembled in the mind by an active reader. What is important for us here is the response expected of the public: instead of passively listening to the building speak a familiar language, it must actively read or decode meaning. Moreover, Labrouste's signs, Levine argues, were specific, only comprehensible in the context of their use in that building. In this way, Labrouste made architecture the vehicle for highly personal and complex thought, "something to be outlined by the architect and read by the public." For Levine, Duc's facade and vestibule were a deliberate repudiation of Labrouste's library, for their orders and plasticity reanimated architecture with tenuous anthropomorphic and declamatory powers—so as to make it easier to understand.[190]

As we have seen, the partially declamatory aspect of the criminal courts wing was not easy for the public to understand, but did draw the public into the act of interpretation and judgment. Nor did critics miss the peculiar and fragmented use of its classical elements. Indeed, Duc's architecture seemed to contemporaries to exude psychological character, something different from the anthropomorphic, corporal quality that traditional classical architecture was thought to have embodied.[191] Duc's rare forays into writing confirm that he worried that the liberty available to the modern artist eroded the common ground necessary for a public imagery, and that he sought that common ground precisely through highly personal architectural detailing.[192] His strategy appears to have been two-fold: to encourage the viewer's empathetic projection into details, and to use elements and types with preexisting associations to draw the public into the specific content of the building. What this qualified animation of architecture achieves, perhaps, is a discursive iconicity—it enlarges the architecture beyond the personal idea of the architect to accommodate a range of meanings and to engage the judgment of the public.

By situating Duc's work in the larger social context of use and reception, and even dissociating it from its architect, we have considered the significance of another aspect of publicity for modern architecture: not only the reading public, but also the persistently live public.[193] The criminal courts wing could be said to have transposed the challenge of architectural legibility to a physically present and implicated public, a process of confrontation that entailed reading into well-lit material shapes and surfaces the kinesthetic and psychological qualities of gesture and expression—severity, stiffness, and resistance; elasticity and compliance—which were as important to the theory and reception of modern art and architecture as to the discourse of social sciences such as criminology. Hence the plasticity of the courtroom ceiling, of Bonnat's crucified corpse, of Duc's prefatory orders in the facade and waiting hall, and the thematization of the light that reveals plasticity, for as Cruppi observed, "the impression made upon the jury by a given declaration almost always results from the exterior appearance, the *plasticity* of the testimony."[194]

In exploring iconicity over text, this essay has taken up that observation made but not pursued by Foucault, that the spectacle of justice shifted in the post-Revolutionary period from the scene of punishment to that of judgment. A brief return to the question of why and how Foucault avoided its analysis may help to clarify, by way of conclusion, the strategy and implications of this essay. Foucault's writings suggest that he saw in the trial a mixture of the spectacle of sovereignty and disciplinary surveillance that threatened to compromise his crucial distinction between the two. To sustain that distinction, Foucault argued that spectacle was a thing of the past, an anachronistic "mask" for modern disciplinary power, one that would wither away if we could avert our gaze.[195] That metaphor creates an obstacle to an analysis of the interplay between the two modes of power. Yet the way that Foucault posited both disciplinary surveillance and sovereignty in visual terms underplays the distinction he made between them. Sovereignty, in Foucault's terms, entails visual display in plastic form, whereas surveillance dissolves plastic display into spatial distribution, and the object of vision into subject, and exchangeable or delegable power into the play of a noncommodifiable gaze. For Foucault, both forms of vision were politically "dangerous," although in different ways:[196] modern sovereign display was dangerous precisely because it could delude the citizen into thinking that he or she actually "held" power, whereas the disciplinary gaze was dangerous because it was difficult to grasp, and because its guise of piercing knowledge and self-knowledge could in effect constitute the individual as a subject, far from assuring his or her power as a citizen. Among other commentators, Martin Jay has pursued this argument to suggest that Foucault construed vision as a prison house (whether dungeon or panopticon) as powerful as language itself, and found no exit. That redemptive option that Jay holds out, of some form of embodied vision, seems not to have been plausible to Foucault because of his investment as a Frenchman in the completion of revolutionary regicide (as Foucault said, we still have not cut off the head of the king), as well as in acknowledging the rise of a political economy that dematerialized products into processes of production and circulation.[197] Even while critiquing its utopian claims, Foucault thus embraced the accompanying Enlightenment ideal: the project of transparent dematerialization.

To account for the revival of the plastic and theatrical in the modern period, such as the one described here as taking place in architectural and social form, I have argued that the techniques at stake in what Foucault called surveillance and spectacle were tied to problems of the visual that are implicit in the inheritance of the paradoxical Enlightenment ideal—a spectacle of transparency. To elaborate that paradox, I have explored a difference in the techniques employed in the courtroom by its various protagonists, above all, the implications of written procedure available to the magistrate who inherited the mantle of the inquisitorial tradition (which Foucault saw as a prototype for modern disciplinary power), and of oral procedure open to the public with its concomitant aspect of eye-witness testimony. I have argued that the latter merits as much attention as the other mode of modern publicity, which is publication, and that it entails both a new form of sovereignty and its own micropolitics. Here I would press Foucault's own point that such systems are not intrinsically evil, but rather, volatile and hence "dangerous." What this account suggests is not only a historical confrontation and mutual infusion of different modalities of representation, which explicitly engage transparency, but the difficulty for the modern historian or critic of isolating a disciplinary transparency from ideological rhetoric. This exploration of representation in both the political and architectural senses suggests that both realms of representation operated in relatively visible *and* immaterial forms.

To take this argument from the social-political-cultural realm into the specifically architectural one, I have also argued that historians cannot sustain the kind of separation that Foucault at times seemed to suggest, between the materiality of architecture displayed in facades and decor, and the immaterial but zoned space of the interiors and exterior environs of post-Enlightenment architecture.[198] Spatial distribution and facades, walls, and decor need to be considered in tandem, and in relation to the social institutions housed and represented by a given building. Moreover, we need to examine public architecture that was meant to visually represent public power, as well as public institutions in which display was chastened, such as the early 19th-century prison and asylum, and buildings of the private domain, namely housing.

Finally, the case of the courthouse has more than anecdotal significance for this enterprise because it engages the modern representation of power at what Foucault described as its core—law—in an arena of resistance to the law and in a situation that fuses public and private. For that infusion of the private and invisible into the public and apparent, which Foucault mapped as the displacement of material observation and display by viewing as immaterial process and piercing insight, was not only evident but also enacted in the representational public institution of the courtroom, which assured a range of roles for the public—as defendant, juror, observer-at-large. These issues have led me to plastically embodied subjects and objects of vision, as well as to a variant on the notion of modern spectacle for which Foucault had little patience. But in insisting, like historians of painting as once-disparate as T. J. Clark and Michael

Fried, on the renewed importance of a theatrical iconicity in the Paris of the 1860s, I have also emphasized its new disembodied conditions, particularly the central problem of how public architecture might represent or interpret publicity and authority where post-Revolutionary ideology requires that authority be diffused or internalized in individualized conscience.[199]

NOTES

1. On the model of the public sphere as the reading public, formed in the Enlightenment, see Jürgen Habermas, *The Structural Transformation of the Public Sphere: An Inquiry into a Category of Bourgeois Society*, trans. T. Burger from the German ed. of 1962 (Cambridge, MA: MIT Press, 1989), in which the reading public, dispersed and abstract in nature, functions as the condition for authentic legislative government or democracy. In this scheme, any iconicity or "staged publicity" poses the political danger of "feudalism" (a version of the false consciousness from which the literate bourgeois culture is somehow protected despite its acknowledged contradictions), which has recurred through the agency of mass media, especially in the age of film and television. See especially 2–26, 159–175, 200–201, 206–207. For a more recent affirmation of Habermas' stand against representational art and the values he associates with it: "Modernism—An Incomplete Project," (1980) reprinted in Hal Foster, ed., *The Anti-Aesthetic: Essays on Postmodern Culture* (Port Townsend, WA: Bay Press, 1983). Within the recent field of studies of Enlightenment culture as the basis for a republic of letters in which texts and symbols displace icons, Sarah Maza has explored this idea specifically in relation to the discourse of the pre-Revolutionary French courts. In several fine articles analyzing late 18th-century lawyers' briefs, Maza has laid the basis for a forthcoming book which argues that the briefs demonstrate a melodramatic literary style that enabled the intersection of private and public spheres, with all its political implications: "Le Tribunal de la nation: les mé-moires judiciaires et l'opinion publique à la fin de l'Ancien Régime," *Annales ESC* (January-February 1987): 73–90; "The Rose-Girl of Salency: Representations of Virtue in Prerevolutionary France," *Eighteenth-Century Studies* 22 (1989): 395–412; "Domestic Melodrama as Political Ideology: The Case of the Comte de Sanois," *American Historical Review* 94 (December 1989): 1249–1264. From the point of view of the 19th century, however, this phenomenon anticipated in textual form what developed in iconic theatrical form in the criminal courtroom itself, once the legal system was overhauled at the turn of the century.

2. This essay began as a lecture in a symposium on the monumental form of Paris held at Northwestern University's Block Gallery in January 1991; its purpose was to insert the issue of the institutional life of Paris into the consideration of monumentality as topography. Elsewhere I have analyzed the criminal courts wing and the 19th-century modernization of the Palais as a whole from the point of view of its physical design and production: "Le Code et l'équité: la transformation du Palais de Justice de Paris au XIXe siècle," in *La Justice en ses temples. Regards sur l'architecture judiciaire en France* (Poitiers: Brissaud, forthcoming); "The Palais de Justice of Paris: Modernization, Historical Self-Consciousness, and their Prehistory in French Institutional Architecture," Ph.D. diss., Harvard University, 1989. The present essay forms part of an exploration of the social character of the building, not only in terms of its critical reception, but also the mediation of its creation and reception through its use. My

109

book, *Modernizing the Palais de Justice: Architecture and Justice in Nineteenth-Century Paris*, to be published by the Architectural History Foundation/MIT Press, will look at the rebuilding of the Palais as a kind of portraiture of a social institution in the making, whose component jurisdictions and complementary institutions were each individually as well as conjointly experienced and conceptualized by its architects, patrons, and publics. Apart from their thematic argument, these studies constitute the first systematic history of the post-Revolutionary modernization of the Palais based on archival sources. Beyond mention in surveys and guidebooks, the modern Palais has only twice received attention from 20th-century architectural historians, whose comments, focused on the west entrance, are germane to this essay and are noted in the third part of this work.

3. The Morgue was as popular a place for visitation as was the criminal courtroom; it exercised the same skill of visual scrutiny to discover identity—as will be seen in Troppmann's trial. The *Revue municipale* (April 16, 1855): 1441, acknowledged the practice as an aspect of contemporary fascination with physiognomic interpretation when it asserted, in an article on the Morgue, that *morgue* was an old French term for face. On the Morgue's popularity, see Allan Mitchell, "The Paris Morgue as a Social Institution in the Nineteenth Century," *Francia* 4 (1976): 581–596; Vanessa Schwartz is pursuing this issue in her dissertation for the History Department of the University of California at Berkeley.

4. Due to a revival by historians in the 1980s, particularly Michelle Perrot, the Troppmann case is again well-known. My purpose here is to use the instance of the Troppmann trial to focus attention on a still-neglected aspect of that case and of 19th-century judicial history: the way the case was mediated by the institutional struc-

ture and dynamics of the trial. For recent discussions of Troppmann, see the provocative article by Michelle Perrot, "L'Affaire Troppmann (1869)," *L'Histoire* 30 (January 1981): 28–37, and "Correspondance: l'affaire Troppmann," *L'Histoire* 31 (June 1981): 105, and the comprehensive, more journalistic account by Pierre Drachline, *Le Crime de Pantin: L'Affaire Troppmann* (Paris: Denoël, 1985). Also note: [René Poirier?], "L'Affaire Troppmann," *Le Journal de France* 62 (June 23, 1970): 1722–1723; Guy Le Halle, "Crimes et criminels célèbres de Paris d'autrefois. 1869: Troppmann," *Paris aux cent villages* 42 (March 1979), verso of cover page. This literature has relied heavily on 19th-century press coverage for its structure and content. Certainly the case was deeply conditioned by the nature of the press at that historical moment, and thus by literacy. On this, see especially Perrot, "Fait divers et histoire au XIXe siècle: Note critique (deux expositions)," *Annales ESC* 38 (July-August 1983): 911–919, and the exhibition catalogues in question: Alain Monestier for the Musée national des arts et traditions populaires, *Le Fait divers* (Paris: Réunion des musées nationaux, 1982), and Jean-Pierre Seguin, *Les Canards illustrés du XIXe siècle* (Paris: Bibliothèque nationale, c. 1983). However, the significance of the press should not blind historians to the socio-historical significance of the live spectacle of the trial, an aspect that the press sought to communicate.

It is clear that the rekindling of historical interest in the sensational trial owes much to its fascination currently. American television, as I write in April 1991, supports five serial programs on the subject; French television coverage of the Gulf war in January of 1991, itself an extraordinary media event, competed with coverage of Simone Weber's trial for murder; and Natalie Zemon Davis, *Fiction in the Archives: Pardon Tales and their Tellers in 16th-Century France* (Stanford:

such subjects

110

Stanford University Press, 1987), viii, acknowledges thinking of her work on the 16th-century pardon tale in relation to the self-defense of Jean Harris and Bernard Goetz in the current news. This renewed fascination surely has to do with the qualities of "secondary orality" that Walter J. Ong attributes to the age of electronic media: *Orality and Literacy: The Technologizing of the Word* (London: Methuen, 1982), 135–138, and which pose anew issues of the trial as a presentational genre.

5. Richard Harbinger, "Trial by Drama," *Judicature* 55 (October 1971): 122–128. Although Harbinger was commenting on American trials, his point is relevant to the French system as well.

6. The classic general text on French criminal justice and its procedure remains Adhémar Esmein, *A History of Continental Criminal Procedure, with Special Reference to France*, revised by the author from the French ed. of 1882, with added sections by François Garraud, trans. John Simpson (Boston: Little, Brown and Company, 1913). It is characteristic of traditional French legal history in that it focuses on the prehistory and establishment of the modern system during the Revolutionary and Napoleonic periods and treats the system as an essentially static affair thereafter, noting debates and reforms during the 19th century as a string of isolated, essentially non-destabilizing events. For a roughly contemporaneous, comparative explanation of French criminal procedure to Americans, see James Garner, "Criminal Procedure in France," *Yale Law Journal* 25 (February 1916): 255–284. As Renée Martinage wrote as recently as 1989, "l'histoire du droit pénal depuis le XIXe reste à écrire": *Punir le crime. La Répression judiciaire depuis le code pénal* (Villeneuve d'Ascq: l'Espace juridique, 1989), 11. Martinage's book is a step in this direction, archivally documenting the effects of judicial practice, that is, the

pattern of verdicts in capital crimes tried in the Department of the Nord between 1811 and 1950; however, a synthetic history of the social and judicial processes that fostered the effects is still needed.

7. On the displacement of spectacle from punishment to trial, see Michel Foucault, *Discipline and Punish: the Birth of the Prison*, orig. pub. 1975, trans. Alan Sheridan (New York: Vintage Books, 1979), 9. Foucault discusses the sovereign-cum-disciplinary character of judgment in *Discipline and Punish*, esp. 216–228, as well as in the "Two Lectures" given a year later, published in Foucault, *Power/Knowledge: Selected Interviews and Other Writings, 1972–1977*, ed. Colin Gordon (New York: Pantheon, 1980), 78–108. The latter could function as an explanation of why Foucault did not analyze trial proceedings in themselves. For while it is true that he and his students explored the case history of a particular trial, in Foucault, ed., *I, Pierre Rivière, having slaughtered my mother, my sister, and my brother. . .: A Case of Parricide in the Nineteenth Century*, orig. pub. 1973, trans. Frank Jellinek (New York: Pantheon, 1975), they focused on its textual aspects at the expense of the dynamics of courtroom procedure. The spectacularity of the latter Foucault viewed as distracting attention from the primary issue of the (written) judicial investigation, which was disciplinary in nature, and whose long institutional history provided a prototype for the Enlightenment invention of disciplinary techniques that reconstituted modern life in more far-reaching ways—causing prototypically magisterial discipline and juridical sovereignty to bifurcate (*Discipline and Punish*, 225, 227).

8. It is not accidental that such an influential form of the critique of Enlightenment humanitarian discourse, though applicable to the welfare state in general, was developed by a Frenchman, given the persistence of the French tradition of magisterial au-

thority in the modern period. Initially, historians inspired by Foucault to study the repressive system concentrated like him on the prison; in the 1980s, historical interest broadened to include the trial. Interestingly, it is an American historian unconcerned with the Foucauldian perspective, yet aroused by the authority of the French magistrate, who has provided the major historical discussion of modern French criminal justice as a system: Benjamin Martin, *Crime and Criminal Justice under the Third Republic: The Shame of Marianne* (Baton Rouge: Louisiana State University Press, 1990), chaps. 4 and 5, esp. 177–184. Building on his earlier study, *The Hypocrisy of Justice in the Belle Epoque* (Baton Rouge: Louisiana State University Press, 1984), Martin's chief finding is that modern French justice was itself criminal because it failed to root out the inquisitorial tradition (*Crime*, 274). In short, he condemns the French system by Anglo-American accusatorial standards taken as universal ethical values. (For an explanation of these terms, see the text below.) For a briefer but richer account of French criminal procedure in the late 19th century, emphasizing the way the system served the peculiarly French emphasis on the psychology of the defendant, see Ruth Harris, *Murders and Madness: Medicine, Law and Society in the Fin de Siècle* (Oxford: Clarendon Press, 1989), 125–138. Also see Robert Nye, *Crime, Madness, and Politics in Modern France: The Medical Concept of National Decline* (Princeton: Princeton University Press, 1984), a work that also exemplifies recognition of turn-of-the-century French jurists' reconceptualizations of modern criminal justice, in the context of the late 20th-century interest in social deviance, which Foucault helped to establish. The specifically French rationales for criminal procedure are precisely what interest me here, for they offer the ideological bases for representations and disputes over representations of authority in modern French jus-

tice. French publications from the late 1970s and 1980s have contributed important studies of the socio-political milieux and experience of particular protagonists, from magistrates and lawyers to jurors and defendants; citations are given in subsequent notes. These tend, however, to focus on isolated types of participants and not to include the courtroom public. The synthesis of those studies with the history of procedure and courtroom practice is still to be developed.

9. This aspect has been acknowledged but insufficiently explored by historians. See most recently Edward Berenson, *The Trial of Madame Caillaux* (Berkeley & Los Angeles: University of California Press, 1992). The spectacularity of that 1914 trial served the author primarily as a springboard into a social history (a microhistory) developed around the protagonists and their testimony—the reverse or complement of the emphasis here, which favors analysis of the proceedings over the content of the Troppmann case. There exists one exceptional study of French judicial ritual in itself, by the magistrate and jurist Antoine Garapon, *L'Ane portant des reliques. Essai sur le rituel judiciaire* (Paris: Centurion, 1985). I am most grateful to Robert Jacob and Nadine Marchal-Jacob for introducing me to this work and its author. Garapon's structuralist method and premises, however, reinforce the traditional message of studies by French jurists—the timelessness of the judicial system and its values—rather than inscribing ritual in a historically specific and dynamic context.

10. François Garraud, "The Different Types of Criminal Procedure," in Esmein, 3–12; for a historical explanation of these models and their rationales, see Esmein's text. On the pre-Revolutionary penal procedure, see also André Langui and Arlette Lebigre, *Histoire du droit pénal*, vol. 2: *La Procédure criminelle* (Paris: Cujas, 1979), and

for a Second Empire account of it, Charles Berriat-Saint-Prix, *Des tribunaux et de la procédure du grand criminel au XVIIIe siècle jusqu'en 1789* (Paris: Auguste Aubry, 1859).

11. This signed but undated work has been estimated as "1858/62" by Provost; it was included in the Daumier exhibition at Durand-Ruel in 1878, shortly before the artist's death. See K. E. Maison, *Honoré Daumier, Catalogue Raisonné of the Paintings, Watercolours and Drawings*, 2 vols., (London: Thames and Hudson, 1968), 2: #680; Louis Provost, *Honoré Daumier: A Thematic Guide to the Oeuvre*, ed. Elizabeth Childs (New York & London: Garland, 1989), 217.

12. For comments testifying to the normative status of civil law and the marginality of criminal law and practice, see Jean Cruppi, *La Cour d'assises* (Paris: Calmann Lévy, 1898), 124–126; André Damien, *Les Avocats du temps passé* (Versailles: H. Lefebvre, 1973), 275, 362.

13. Sources for particular aspects of procedure will be noted below. In general, on the Second Empire's criminal procedure, see Charles Nouguier, *La Cour d'assises. Traité pratique*, 5 vols. (Paris: Cosse, Marchal, 1868). Nouguier was a judge in the criminal section of the Supreme Court or Cour de cassation, which ruled on petitions to quash verdicts of the Cour d'assises. His manual is important as a guide not merely to procedural code, but to how that code was observed and enforced in practice as of 1868. On the Second Empire's misdemeanors procedure, see Charles Berriat-Saint-Prix, *Traité de la procédure des tribunaux criminels*, part 2 (Paris: Cosse, 1851–1857). For 19th-century civil procedure in general, see Albert Tissier, *Le Centenaire du code de procédure et les projets de réforme* (Paris: Sirey, 1906). In many respects the French courts still follow the system established by the Napoleonic codes, but changes have been gradually implemented, and the codes were

themselves overhauled in 1958 (penal procedure) and 1975 (civil procedure). On the code of penal procedure currently in effect, see Roger Merle and André Vitu, *Traité de droit criminel*, vol. 2: *Procédure pénale*, 4th ed. (Paris: Cujas, 1979).

14. Nouguier, 3: 246–48. The code is ambiguous in this regard; Nouguier points out that the standard interpretation was that judges could dispense with witnesses if they felt that there was definitive evidence in other forms.

15. Garraud, in Esmein, 3, 11–12; Esmein, 528–529. For a history of French debate and legislation concerning the political and judicial status of the jury from its Revolutionary origin into the 20th century, see Bernard Schnapper, "Le jury français aux XIX et XX siècles," in Antonio Schioppa, ed., *The Trial Jury in England, France, Germany 1700–1900*, Comparative Studies in Continental and Anglo-American Legal History, ed. Helmut Coing and Knut Norr, vol. 4 (Berlin: Duncker & Humblot, 1987), 165–239. Eugène Lambert, *Philosophie de la Cour d'Assises* (Paris: Plon, 1861), is an instance of a judge who viewed the code in sacral terms; Cruppi is an instance of a magistrate who acknowledged the function of equity in jury verdicts despite his general suspicion of jury trials, 250, and Schnapper, 190, cites a statement of that view in print as early as 1830. I am grateful to Colin Lucas for his reflections on the way the criminal system could be seen to implement modern sovereignty.

Concerning popular fascination with the juried criminal courts, see the comment of Judge Brouchot quoted by Robert Vouin, "La Cour d'assises française de 1808 à 1958," in Institut de droit comparé de l'Université de Paris, *Problèmes contemporains de procédure pénale. Recueil d'études en hommage à M. Louis Hugueney* (Paris: Sirey, 1964), 226: "[La Cour d'assises] est à peu près la seule, sinon la seule des juridictions françaises à laquelle ce qu'il est convenu d'appeler le grand public porte quelque intérêt."

16. Walter J. Ong, *Orality and Literacy* (London: Methuen, 1982), 31–116, 139–155. It should be noted that Ong argues for a fundamental difference between orality, which he associates with hearing, gesture and action (although the latter are of course observed), and literacy, which he associates with vision, because on the printed page language becomes visualizable; that argument runs counter to the iconicity/textuality opposition noted earlier. I do not subscribe to Ong's distinction in applying his observations to the trial, because there orality was closely associated with vision, as shall be demonstrated.

17. Fig. 11 represents the same chief courtroom of the Paris Palais that is shown in earlier states in figs. 1 and 2. On the Supreme Court justices, see Maxime Du Camp, *Paris, ses organes, ses fonctions et sa vie dans la seconde moitié du XIXe siècle*, 6 vols., 6th ed. of vol. 3, orig. pub. 1872 (Paris: Hachette, 1879), 3: 151, reprinted from his article "Le Palais de Justice à Paris: La Cour d'assises," *Revue des deux mondes* 82 (August 15, 1869): 852: "Ils ne s'inquiètent ni du crime commis, ni de la personne des condamnés. Ils sont au-dessus des choses humaines et ne prononcent que sur des abstractions."

18. Ong, 31–77, and esp. 139–155; Peter Brooks, *The Melodramatic Imagination: Balzac, Henry James, Melodrama and the Mode of Excess* (New Haven: Yale University Press, 1976), passim.

19. Cruppi, 86–90; Henri Berr, "Ce qu'est le jury criminel; ce qu'il devrait être: notes et réflexions d'un juré," *Revue politique et parlementaire* 53 (September 1907): 483–509, esp. 496.

20. Fig. 12 shows London's criminal courtroom circa 1844. On the lack of public prosecutor in Britain, see Garraud, in Es-mein, 571, 598, but cf. John Langbein, "The English Criminal Trial Jury," in Schioppa, ed., *The Trial Jury*, 19–22; also see Cruppi, 48.

21. This central arena was described in the 19th century as the *barreau*, meaning an area set off from the public by a barrier, in which witnesses and lawyers addressed the judges—hence the transfer of the term to the corporation of locally accredited lawyers, the bar or *barreau*. A rarer 19th-century synonym for the architectural meaning of *barreau* was the *parquet*. Historically, the term *parquet* derived from the ancien régime courtroom, where the prosecutor made his speeches from the floor, addressing the judges seated on benches that enclosed the floor or *parquet* on two sides (fig. 1). His profession was known as the *magistrature debout*, in distinction to the judges, the *magistrature assise*. Ironically in the 19th century, the prosecutor spoke from the judges' bench, abandoning the physical space of the *parquet* to the lawyers and witnesses. Although the prosecution staff and its offices came to be known metonymically as the *parquet*, the term *barreau* superseded it in the courtroom itself, for now apparent reasons. Occasionally the global term *prétoire*, referring to the courtroom as a whole, seems to have been used to refer to the central arena, as in Bérard des Glajeux, *Souvenirs d'un président d'assises (1880–1890)*, 2 vols. (Paris: Plon, 1892–93), 1: 223; Presse judiciaire parisienne, *Le Palais de Justice de Paris. Son monde et ses moeurs* (Paris: Ancienne maison Quantin, 1892), 151, 277; also Harrap's French to English dictionary, which specifies a juridical usage of *prétoire* as the floor of the courtroom. For the 19th- and early 20th-century definition of *barreau*, see the Caisse nationale de recherche scientifique, *Trésor de la langue française. Dictionnaire de la langue du XIXe et du XXe siècle (1789–1960)* (Paris: Gallimard, 1986). On the etymology of *parquet*, see Du Camp, *Paris*, 3:

151–152. A different term for this area was offered by Garapon writing in the 1980s: he baptizes it *le cancel*, the chancel, to underscore the dependence of courtroom organization on church architecture, and the restricted access to this area which accords it a quasi-sacred status (30–32, 34).

22. See Cruppi, 165, regarding the suspicion of the bar which gave rise to "article 311 du Code d'Instruction criminelle, qui chaque jour encore, au début de l'audience, donne lieu à la Cour d'assises à un manège singulier. Le défenseur se soulève à demi sur son banc, et, inclinant la tête, il reçoit du président . . . l'avertissement 'de ne rien dire contre sa conscience ou contre le respect dû aux lois, de s'exprimer avec décence et modération'." Other commentators complained of the redundancy of this provision, whose effect, Cruppi said, was to "rompre l'égalité entre l'accusation et la défense et traiter celle-ci en suspecte." For instance, Nouguier, 3: 37, observed that the oath reaffirmed yearly by members of the bar already guaranteed the lawyer's professional integrity. What is striking is the ritual insistence upon the provisional status of the lawyer, who was a self-employed professional acting in the interests of individuals, as against the authority of the magistrature, civil servants who in France enjoyed a juridical status distinct from that of individuals.

23. Cruppi, 42–44: "Au combat! c'est bien le mot—ou plutôt au tournoi, à la lutte brillante où, dans l'éclat des passes d'armes, dans le cliquetis joyeux des épées, disparaissent aux yeux du spectateur les deuils qui ont ouvert cette lice, et ceux qu'elle va faire naître. . . . Clinique de théâtre plutôt que d'hôpital; salle propice aux "attitudes" par les belles distances que l'architecte a ménagées entre les acteurs. . . . Le milieu, l'atmosphère, imposent aux personnages qui, par diverses portes, pénètrent dans la brillante salle, quelque chose de la contenance d'artistes prêts à jouer un rôle, et supportant

déjà le feu de tous les regards." Reflecting Cruppi's ideal of medical expertise, this book was his diagnosis of the pathology of the Cour d'assises and his proposal for therapy. It should be noted that Cruppi was not advocating a return to the inquisitorial traditions of the past, but rather was trying to create conditions conducive to expert opinion in court—with the practical effect of infusing the accusatorial hearing of the defendant with a new form of an old tradition of professional authority, knowledge and control. On this, see the second part of this study.

24. Cruppi, 50: "[L]a place est si étroite que si le bras du *barrister* s'abandonnait à quelques gestes, les perruques voisines en seraient sûrement dérangées." For Cruppi's description of the British criminal courtroom, see 45–54. It must be noted, however, that the British were less content with their crowded, dilapidated quarters: at the time of Cruppi's book, they were planning the sumptuous reconstruction of Old Bailey completed in 1907. Cf. W. Eden Hooper, *The History of Newgate and Old Bailey* (London: Underwood Press, 1935), 12, a popular edition based on Hooper's expensive monograph commemorating the inauguration, *The Central Criminal Court of London* (London, 1909).

25. This juxtaposition of architectural types with distinct associations is my gloss, rather than Cruppi's, although French architects thought in terms of types, as evidenced by 19th-century architectural treatises and criticism. I know of one instance in which a popular journalist described a Parisian courtroom in terms of a Protestant temple, using the analogy to imply an inappropriate lack of pomp and dignity: Presse judiciaire, 258. For a recent French analysis of the space of the courtroom in terms of derivation from the basilican Catholic church, see Garapon, 30–31.

London's criminal courtroom of the early

1840s (fig. 12) was variously described as square in [Thomas Hosmer Shepherd, illustrator], *London Interiors: A Grand National Exhibit . . . from drawings made expressly for this work . . . with descriptions written by official authorities*, 2 vols. (London: Joseph Mead, n.d. [1841–44]), 1:95; and as oblong, in *Cruchley's Picture of London* (London: Cruchley, 1846), 258–59. Its earlier form as of 1809 is illustrated as rectangular in Hooper, *The History of Newgate*.

26. This fee was described as "slight" in *Cruchley's Picture of London* of 1846, 259; as "at least one shilling" in the *Handbook to London As It Is* (London, John Murray, 1871), 138, but adjusted upward relative to demand; and as one and a half shillings by 1900 in that year's edition of Karl Baedeker's *London and its Environs* (Leipzig, 1900), 224. This was presumably enough to bar admission to the poor and unemployed, whom the Paris courts grudgingly admitted. David Brownlee, *The Law Courts: The Architecture of George Edmund Street* (Cambridge, MA: The Architectural History Foundation and MIT Press, 1984), has pointed out how the new civil courts in London, inaugurated in 1882, were planned to limit public access—unlike their Paris counterpart. On the competition projects for the building, see 109–111, 119, 134, 145–146; on G. E. Street's building, 176, 222–223, 359.

27. French use of graded benches in 19th-century courtrooms was minimal and limited to the jury box and defendant's dock. Graded seating on a larger scale and galleries for the public were never considered in Paris, except in the chief courtroom of the Cour d'appel, inaugurated in 1891, where a gallery was included because of planning problems unrelated to the courtroom itself, and access was not available to the public: G. Raulin, "Le Palais de Justice de Paris et les nouveaux bâtiments de la Cour d'appel," *L'Architecture* 4 (November 1891): 542. Cases of galleries in provincial courtrooms are rare, and they were never considered a desirable solution to cramped sites or public crowds.

28. As illustrated in the *London Illustrated News* (May 1856): 560.

29. The chief courtroom in the Palais (figs. 1, 2, 11) sits in the upper left quadrant of the plan (fig. 14), sandwiched between the pair of round towers in the north facade and the main waiting hall for the Palais, with its central spine of columns. The new criminal courtrooms occupied the level above the cell blocks of the detention prison indicated on the plan, and replaced the old criminal courtroom located just east (or in the plan, above) the new wing. This general plan of 1869 combines some existing buildings with some projected new sections of the Palais. Thus it also shows an early project for rebuilding the appellate courts at the center of the Palais complex, whereas in 1869 a Gothic wing still stood on the alignment of the wing shown just east of the new criminal wing and contained the old criminal courtroom on the second floor (fig. 57). That structure, already slated for demolition, was badly damaged by fires set during the Commune in 1871 and was razed soon after.

30. An early plan for the development of the rue de Rennes, a major left bank thoroughfare, shows the street arriving at the Seine to feed into the pont neuf; it was published in the *Gazette municipale* (1853). A later plan published in the Département de la Seine, *Documents relatifs aux travaux du Palais de Justice*, text volume and atlas of plates (Paris, 1858), atlas, plate 34, adjusted the route westward and linked it to a proposed new bridge paralleling the pont neuf. When the city finally took up the long-delayed extension of the rue de Rennes in 1911, this bridge (ultimately not built) was discussed as having a T-shape, linked by its stem to the pont neuf and thereby serving the Palais: Eugène Hénard, "Le pont neuf

et la pointe de la Cité," *L'Architecture* 24 (1911): 108, plate 29. The new west entrance of the Palais, with its monumental stair and its environs offering partial visibility from the river banks and the *terre-plein* of the pont neuf, was only completed and put into use in 1875.

31. From the start of modernization work at the Palais in 1835, plans had called for two courtrooms for the criminal courts or Cour d'assises, to permit two simultaneous sessions. Two courtrooms with the same facilities and decorative character were in fact built. However, the Second Empire's relationship to the criminal courts was ambivalent; even while constructing accessible and theatrical quarters, the government inaugurated a policy of "correctionalization" that effectively diverted some of the case load from the criminal courts. On this practice, see note 141. Consequently only one criminal courtroom was needed. The north courtroom, which is the one we shall examine here, was put into use for the Cour d'assises; the south courtroom was inaugurated by the appellate chamber for the misdemeanors courts, a chamber that did not use a jury, but did require some of the facilities provided for a criminal courtroom. See A. Sorel, "Inauguration de nouvelles salles au Palais-de-Justice," *Le Droit* (November 5, 1868): 1078.

32. The virtue of a special entrance to the criminal courts which was partially isolated from the rest of the Palais is nicely phrased by Oscar Rigaud, "La restauration du Palais de Justice," *L'Illustration* 52 (1868): 298: "[L]a salle des Pas-Perdus . . . est spacieuse et grandiose. . . . Aux jours des grands procès, le Palais tout entier ne sera plus, comme autrefois, envahi par la foule, et les travaux des autres Chambres ne seront plus troublés par les cris, les disputes, le va et vient des spectateurs impatients d'entrer et faisant queue du matin au soir dans l'attente d'une place qu'ils n'obtiennent pas."

33. Figures for the capacity of the courtroom as modified for Troppmann's trial and details on the policing of the crowd are cited by Thomas Grimm in *Le Petit journal* (December 29, 1869): 1, and in the *Gazette des tribunaux* (December 29, 1869).

34. "Le public est bien tranché: aux bancs réservés les dentelles, ici les mouchoirs bleus; là-bas le parfum de l'héliotrope, ici le relent du saucisson à l'ail. . . ": Presse judiciaire, 278.

35. Drachline, 103. Drachline's is a recent anecdotal account of the case, based on 19th-century sources but unfootnoted. Félix Sangnier, *Plaidoyers de Charles Lachaud*, 2 vols. (Paris: G. Charpentier, 1885), 2: 258, estimates a modest 3,000. Bérard, 1: 234, wrote that requests for invitations to sensational trials ranged between six and seven hundred; Troppmann's trial, however, was exceptional even in the category of sensational trials.

36. *Le Petit journal* (December 25, 1869): 2; (January 1, 1870): 1; on tickets changing hands, Bérard, 1: 225; on courtesans and for indication of his own presence, see Du Camp, *Paris*, 3: 172–74; for biographical details, L. G. Vapereau, *Dictionnaire universel des contemporains*, 4th ed. (Paris: Hachette, 1870). On the types of people who generally requested tickets, see Bérard, 1: 170–171, who cited writers like Wolf and Meilhac, actors like the Théâtre français's Coquelin, military intellectuals like Colonel Lichtenstein, professors like Doctor Peter, artists like the Belgian painter Alfred Stevens, journalists like Ganderax, and lawyers like Charles Garnier, Gérôme, Paul Laurens and Machard.

37. Nouguier, 3: 11–12; Bérard, 1: 240–241.

38. Middle-class association of the working class with the danger of crime, pointed out in a classic account by Louis Chevalier, *Laboring Classes and Dangerous Classes in Paris During the First Half of the Nineteenth*

Century, orig. pub. Paris, 1958, trans. Frank Jellinek (New York: Howard Fertig, 1973), gave way to a focus on dangerous types of individuals later in the century, as Robert Nye has noted (citing Pierre Sorlin) in *Crime*, 181. Luc Passion has argued that, statistically, poverty was a declining factor in Second Empire crime such that "le fossé se creuse entre 'la classe dangereuse et la classe laborieuse'": "Conjoncture et géographie du crime à Paris sous le Second Empire," *Mémoires publiés par la Fédération des sociétés historiques et archéologiques de Paris et de l'Ile de France* 33 (1982): 186–224, esp. 221.

39. Du Camp, *Paris*, 3: 172; Bérard, 1: 224 ("les rangs populaires où les individus jugés ont toujours un grand nombre de partisans qui ne cachent pas leurs impressions"), 240–241; also note Bérard's worry that without a ticket system, spectators from the populace would monopolize the public area, for the ushers would surreptitiously admit spectators to the enclosed benches, such that seated and standing spectators would be "tous de même origine, se donnant la main par-dessus la balustrade qui les sépare" and would constitute "pour l'accusé un parterre d'adversaires ou de partisans" (241).

40. Bérard, 1: 224–225: "Il avait ses moeurs, ses traditions, sa jurisprudence, son point de vue indépendant, et agissait efficacement, soit pour contrôler les impressions de la presse judiciaire, soit pour prévenir chez les jurés très sensibles aux appréciations des leurs, présents à l'audience, les velléités des à-coups. C'étaient les jurés du dehors."

41. "Des personnes étrangères aux habitudes judiciaires, avides d'émotions, et cherchant avant tout à satisfaire leur curiosité, ont été admises près de la cour. C'est là un véritable abus: la foule qui, lorsqu'un grand procès l'attire, se presse dans l'enceinte réservée, rend plus difficile la police de l'audience et peut troubler les témoins. Peut-être même est-il à craindre que les sentiments qu'elle manifeste pour ou contre l'accusé ne réagissent quelquefois sur le jury et n'influent sur ses décisions." Ministère de la justice, *Receuil officiel des instructions et circulaires du Ministère de la justice, publié par les ordres du Garde des sceaux, Ministre de la justice*, 3 vols. (Paris, 1879–1883), 2 (covering 1841–1862): 72.

42. "Cette manière de procéder . . . est de nature à entraîner de graves inconvénients; elle peut modifier le caractère que doivent toujours conserver les audiences judiciaires, et porter ainsi atteinte à la dignité de la justice; elle pourrait exposer en outre les magistrats à d'injustes critiques." Ministère de la justice, *Bulletin officiel du Ministère de la justice. Décrets, arrêtés, circulaires, décisions, année 1886* (Paris, published annually 1876–1919), 225.

43. The controversial problem of the dependence of the magistrature on the regime in power, which led the French public to question the impartiality of its professional judges, is discussed further below in relation to the magistrature's entrance into the courtroom. For texts of the sequence of charters and constitutions which specify the source of sovereignty and the name in which justice will be rendered, see Charles Debrasch and Jean-Marie Pontier, *Les Constitutions de la France* (Paris: Dalloz, 1983), esp. art. 57 of the Charter of 1814, and arts. 5, 7, and 9 of Louis-Napoléon's constitution of 1852, which provided the basis for the Second Empire proclaimed at the end of that year. The magistrature accordingly swore a personal oath of loyalty to Louis-Napoléon at the Elysées palace on April 4, 1852, pointedly superseding that Republican oath of loyalty to personal conscience that it had sworn in unprecedented public pomp "devant les hommes" at the Palais de Justice in 1849: *Moniteur universel* (November 4, 1849 & April 6, 1852). Summary explanation of the ancien régime doctrine of

royal justice, as delegated to professional magistrates and as retained by the monarch, is available in François Olivier-Martin, *Histoire du droit français des origines à la Révolution* (Paris: Domat Montchrestien, 1948), book 2, and manuals of institutional history such as Jacques Ellul, *Histoire des institutions* (Paris: PUF, 1962), 3: 316; for a study of retained justice in practice—royal pardons and pleas for them—see Davis, *Fiction*. On the elimination of the right of pardon during the Revolutionary period, see Charles Berriat-Saint-Prix, *Le Jury en matière criminelle. Manuel des jurés à la cour d'assises*, 4th rev. ed. (Paris: Cosse, Marchal, 1867), 137.

44. For a sage discussion of truth, fiction, and the narrative shaping of evidence in the context of criminal charges, see Davis, *Fiction*, "Introduction," 1–6.

45. Jan Goldstein, *Console and Classify: The French Psychiatric Profession in the Nineteenth Century* (Cambridge, England: Cambridge University Press, 1987; paperback ed., 1990), 91–94. As Goldstein points out, Pinel developed the technique of theatrical spectacles to persuade patients, at the level of imagination rather than reason, that they could abandon certain delusions—for instance, delusions of guilt. That mock trials were prominent among these therapeutic spectacles is another indication of how oral trials were associated with imagination and impressions. The importance of trials within a popular oral culture is signalled by the 18th-century mock trial (ironically, staged by printers) analyzed by Robert Darnton, *The Great Cat Massacre and Other Episodes in French Cultural History* (New York: Basic Books, 1984), chap. 2.

It is important to emphasize the implications of the differences between oral and written forms of evidence for the Enlightenment idea that sense impressions informed and were the natural bases of reason. My argument is that written procedure in effect fostered a different kind of reasoning and judgment, more abstract and less contextual, than oral procedure. If the French jury began as an Enlightenment institution, its basis for judgment took on a different aspect by the latter 19th century, when the initially descriptive, positive terms "impression" and "sensation" became pejorative, associated with socially disruptive theatricality. Mona Ozouf's analysis of Revolutionary festivals suggests that such a separation between what were understood to be sensation and reason became evident as early as the Revolutionary period; see note 184.

46. "N'est-ce pas étrange, cette passion folle, cette passion effrénée de femmes élevées dans le velours, les dentelles et la soie; accoutumées à la mièvrerie, aux fadaises et à la frivolité, qu'un rien fait tomber en syncope . . . pour les détails vulgaires et les repugnants débats de bien des causes criminelles!": Thomas Grimm, "Emotions judiciaires," *Le Petit journal* (December 27, 1869): 1; Du Camp, 3: 172.

47. See Harris, esp. 45, 203–207, 228–234, for a general summary of the fin de siècle view, reinforced by the widespread diagnosis of hysteria in women and the high visibility of female crimes of passion in the criminal courts, that women were biologically prone to emotionalism and impulsiveness, which inhibited their capacity for intellectual self-discipline and moral reflection. As Harris points out, 235, at least one Third Republic commentator, Doctor Aubry, proposed that observing trials was liable to inspire women to commit crimes. In short, the public audience and the accused might here too prove interchangeable. Claire Moses, *French Feminism in the Nineteenth Century* (Albany: State University of New York Press, 1984), esp. 45, 93, 132–33, 154–155, 164–167, 188, has pointed out how the polarization of male and female social roles in the 18th century and after, and the ideological attribution of reason primarily to men and emotion primarily to women, were per-

petuated even within the left and among feminists in the course of the 19th century in France. There were, however, protests, for instance, the statement published by the feminist leader Maria Deraismes, in the year of Troppmann's trial: "What women want . . . is that you renounce this arbitrary, fictitious distribution of human faculties that affirms that man represents reason and woman represents emotion" (quoted by Moses, 186).

48. "On comprend en effet, dans de semblables circonstances, l'expansion souvent violente et irrésistible d'un sentiment naturel chez l'homme, plus naturel peut-être encore chez la femme; mais il faut avouer que la présence de dames élégantes et parées aux pieds même du bureau de la Cour, près de la tribune de messieurs les jurés, non loin de l'accusé, a toujours quelque chose de choquant. Elle donne, quoi qu'on puisse dire, l'apparence d'un spectacle indiscret et mondain aux graves et sévères manifestations de la justice." *Gazette des tribunaux* (December 31, 1869). This reporter illustrates for 1869 the claim made by the lawyer Oscar Pinard, *L'Histoire à l'audience 1840–48* (Paris: Pagnerre, 1848), 238–240, that the public of the 1840s, "haletant, hors de lui, emporté" during the debates, typically turned on itself after the verdict to condemn its own unseemly emotion; Pinard declared that the public must now learn to "surveiller sur elle-même" *during* the trial, observing that type of spectacle in respectful silence. Such self-discipline was generally deemed difficult for women. The analogy between behavior ascribed to women and the behavior of the public was made explicit in the Third Republic, in the celebrated studies of the crowd by Gustave LeBon and by the magistrate and criminologist Gabriel Tarde. Tarde wrote: "By its whimsy, its revolting docility, its credulity, its nervousness, its brusque psychological leaps from fury to tenderness, from exasperation to laughter,

the crowd is feminine, even when it is composed, as is usually the case, of males." Cited in Susanna Barrows, *Distorting Mirrors: Visions of the Crowd in Late Nineteenth-Century France* (New Haven: Yale University Press, 1981), 47, 149.

It should be noted that there was no place for women to participate in judging the trial except in the audience. They might be witnesses or defendants, but in the 19th century women were not admitted to juries nor to the legal professions. The first reform came only in 1900, when women were admitted to the bar (Royer, 388), and it was not until World War 1 that female lawyers appeared in numbers on the bench for the defense, as noted by José Théry, "Le Palais de Justice pendant la guerre," *Mercure de France* (July 1, 1915): 466. Female jurors and magistrates are a still more recent occurrence.

49. Du Camp, 3: 172. Women are shown among the most elite visitors sitting behind the magistrates but not in the *barreau* in the illustration of Troppman's trial reproduced in fig. 28.

50. Comparisons to the theater were made by Berriat, *Le Jury*, 89; Du Camp, 3: 172; Presse judiciaire, 277; Cruppi, 43–44, as noted earlier; the comparison was made in a complaint specifically about the Troppmann trial in the legislature in January of 1870, as cited by Drachline, 185. Grimm, in reporting on Troppmann's trial in *Le Petit journal* (December 30 and 31, 1869), invoked the market and the railway station.

51. On the phenomenon of stage seats, banned in 1759–1760 in the two official Paris theaters, see Barbara Mittman, *Spectators on the Paris Stage in the Seventeenth and Eighteenth Centuries*, Theater and Dramatic Studies No. 25 (Ann Arbor: UMI Research Press, 1984). This is an additional context for the argument made by Sara Maza in "Domestic Melodrama," 1260, that during the pre-Revolutionary years, the educated

middle class had come to associate theatricality, and also femininity, with the aristocracy, and truthful sobriety and masculinity with the legal world. In the 19th century, femininity and theatricality were transferred to the crowd. The role of the association between theatricality and femininity in the Enlightenment critique of absolutism, and in the displacement of a theatrical, iconic order by a textual and legalistic ideology is analyzed by Joan Landes, *Women and the Public Sphere in the Age of the French Revolution* (Ithaca: Cornell University Press, 1988), esp. chaps. 2 & 3. For studies of the paradoxical Enlightenment argument that audience interaction with actors promoted a sense of distance from the spectacle on the part of the audience, while a strict physical and behavioral separation between actors and audience promoted audience identification with the spectacle, see note 54.

52. Monestier, 155, notes the relationship between that theater's repertory and the Cour d'assises. For an anecdotal example of lively audience response in the boulevard theaters during the Second Empire, see Georges Cain, *Anciens théâtres de Paris. Le boulevard du Temple, les théâtres du boulevard* (Paris: Charpentier & Fasquelle, 1906), 24–25. Cf., however, Jacques de Plunkett, *Fantômes et souvenirs de la Porte St.-Martin* (Paris: Ariane, 1946), 235–237, who asserts that the audience had become so passive that all response was due to claques. The classic 20th-century recollection of animated theater on the boulevard du Temple (the "boulevard du crime") is the 1945 film by Marcel Carné with screenplay by Jacques Prévert, the script and some stills and notes published as Marcel Carné, *Les Enfants du Paradis (The Children of Paradise)*, Classic Film Scripts (Letchworth, Great Britain: Lorrimer, 1968).

53. See Cruppi, 43, on the courtroom public: "[L]a note dominante, on peut le dire, est la gaîté." It has long been thought

that the young architect Charles Garnier managed to wrest the commission for the new Paris Opéra in 1861 from the sober, imperially backed Viollet-le-Duc, whom the public assumed would receive the job, because Viollet's project was not festive enough or susceptible enough to public promenade and display to represent the contemporary conception of theater. The triumphant Garnier elaborated and articulated this conception in writings, such as his book *Le Théâtre* of 1871, and in his building, whose facade was unveiled in 1867 and which was inaugurated in 1875; his was inevitably a new point of reference for the contemporary definition of theater. For Garnier, theater entailed "a spectacle of pomp and elegance," "luxury and movement" which was the crowd itself as it surged through the building. The spectator was as necessary and active a part of the spectacle as the actor, claimed Garnier, arguing that this fact fostered and justified the arts of self-adornment and self-presentation in audience as in architecture. For a summary interpretation, see David Van Zanten, "Architectural Composition at the Ecole des Beaux-Arts," in Arthur Drexler, ed., *The Architecture of the Ecole des Beaux-Arts* (New York: Museum of Modern Art, 1977), 254–286; also see the full study by Christopher Mead, *Charles Garnier's Paris Opera: Architectural Empathy and the Renaissance of French Classicism* (New York & Cambridge, MA: The Architectural History Foundation and MIT Press, 1991), which, however, gives less emphasis to the social issue of theatricality.

54. Several recent studies have explored Enlightenment theory concerning audience response to theater and painting, as visual phenomena. Thomas Crow, *Painters and Public Life in Eighteenth-Century Paris* (New Haven: Yale University Press, 1985), drawing on John Lough's study of 1957, emphasizes the vociferous, unpredictable response associated with the *parterre*, itself domi-

nated by members of the legal world, and links the *parterre* and the legal world to the emergence of middle-class, art-critical debate which in fact promoted values of sobriety as against aristocratic theatricality (passim, but esp. 14–15). Michael Fried, *Absorption and Theatricality: Painting and Beholder in the Age of Diderot* (Berkeley and Los Angeles: University of California Press, 1980) has posited the foundations of a newly self-conscious contemplative audience response in Diderot's writing. Fried describes the replacement of a direct "theatrical" appeal of character to audience by a dramatic tableau of "absorbed" activity on stage or in a painting, so conceived as to "arrest" the individual spectator in "enthralled" identification (92), in which the spectator experiences a sympathy with the tableau which induces "self-transcendence," causing the audience to lose its identity as an autonomous public (104). Most recently, Scott Bryson has recast Diderot's reconception of audience response as the formation of a bourgeois aesthetic which helps constitute and reinforce the self-discipline necessary to a disciplinary society, instantiating the argument made by Foucault in *Discipline and Punish*. I am grateful to Sarah Maza for alerting me to Bryson's study. In *The Chastised Stage: Bourgeois Drama and the Exercise of Power*, Stanford French and Italian Studies 70 (Saratoga, CA: Anma Libri, 1991), Bryson proposes that this mode prompted its audience to identify with and internalize the new ethical values enacted in theater or painting, distinct from the ethics of the monarchy. He compares the displacement of theatricality by absorption to the contemporaneous replacement of theatrical corporal punishment by imprisonment as interpreted by Foucault, arguing that the value of the latter was to reduce the distance between the criminal and the public to the point that the public could imagine itself in the criminal's position and thus resolve to obey the

law. Yet Bryson notes (44–45, 72) that this process depended on the perception that actor and spectator shared the same middle-class values. It was more difficult to achieve outside the middle class, whether in the theater or in the public criminal courtroom of the 19th century. What continued was the representation of social order in terms specific to the lives of ordinary individuals—the conflation of public and private realms charted by a number of recent scholars. Peter Brooks' study of melodrama has indicated how the subtleties of Diderot's bourgeois drama gave way to starker confrontations of vice and virtue, personified by ordinary characters, in the popular theaters of early 19th-century Paris, with persistent influence among a larger public—as well as in the criminal courtroom (see note 57).

55. On the silence of upper- and middle-class theater audiences as of the 1870s as compared even to those of the 1850s, see Richard Sennett, *The Fall of Public Man* (New York: Random House, 1978), 205–210. Sennett situates this phenomenon, however, in a long development beginning with the removal of stage seats, and the subsequent replacement of the standing-room *parterre* by reserved seats in the new Paris theater of the Comédie française opened in 1782 (74), and argues that the transformation of theater audience from active participants in the 18th century to passive spectators was paralleled in public life at large. For a discussion of the broad trend in the 19th-century criminal courtroom from the silence associated with text-based proceedings to the activity encouraged by oral proceedings (reversing the trend in the theater), see Bérard, 1: 209–216, who begins: "La douceur moutonnière des accusés, l'impassabilité impénétrable du jury, la sévérité régulière des interrogatoires, la marche du débat à pas comptés, tout cela n'est plus dans nos tempéraments judiciaires." The volubility of the courtroom public caused Bérard and others

to describe it as a *parterre* (as quoted in note 39).

56. Du Camp acknowledged the real-life consequences of the trial, implying that this was at once a source of public fascination and a reason to condemn the form it took, 3: 172; also see the Presse judiciaire, 283–284. For another instance conjoining entertainment with the development of skills of interpretation and judgment, see Neil Harris' interpretation of the mid 19th-century American shows of P. T. Barnum: *Humbug: The Art of P. T. Barnum* (Chicago: University of Chicago Press, 1973).

57. Ong's structuralist sketch of the dynamics of orality suggests how orality and publicity could foster melodramatic interpretations of criminal cases in the courtroom, a phenomenon well illustrated by the Troppmann trial; for instance, Ong's emphasis on the mnemonic advantages of grandiose stock characterizations, 69–70, 151–55. The melodramatic form developed in boulevard theaters in the first thirty years of the century was, as Peter Brooks has pointed out (15), historically inscribed and socially instrumental: "[The genre of melodrama] comes into being in a world where the traditional imperatives of truth and ethics have been violently thrown into question, yet where the promulgation of truth and ethics, their instauration as a way of life, is of immediate, daily, political concern. . . . We may legitimately claim that melodrama becomes the principal mode for uncovering, demonstrating, and making operative the essential moral universe in a post-sacred era." But Brooks' claim that the excessive nature of melodrama makes it more persuasive in written than in visual spectacle or performance (108–109) incidentally acknowledges the danger that spectators might come to doubt and reinterpret a melodramatically presented case.

58. For a historical account of fear of the crowd in late 19th-century France, see Barrows, and Robert Nye, *The Origins of Crowd Psychology: Gustave LeBon and the Crisis of the Mass Democracy in the Third Republic* (London and Beverly Hills: Sage Publications, 1975). For an instance of its application to the audience at criminal trials, see Cruppi, 91–92.

59. For example, Petit-Jean, "Courrier du Palais," *Le Monde illustré* (January 1, 1870): 10: "[O]n n'entend rien. Il est vrai qu'en revanche on y voit fort mal"; Du Camp, 3: 864. The placement of the public within the courtroom was frankly interpreted by Rigaud, 298: "Quand on entre dans ces nouvelles salles, on est frappé, sinon de leur petitesse,—elles sont, il est vrai, très-étroites mais très-longues et au demeurant spacieuses,—du moins de la parcimonie avec laquelle la place a été ménagée au public. Un tout petit espace lui est réservé au fond de la salle. . . . C'est une faute que je n'impute pas à l'architecte, mais dont la responsabilité revient à ceux dont il a reçu les ordres. Aurait-on voulu diminuer le nombre des assistants? contrairement au principe de notre loi qui appelle la publicité, qui la commande, qui l'exige, on est enclin, depuis quelques temps, à la restreindre le plus possible. Fâcheuse tendance!"

60. Bérard, 1: 226. The decision of 1891, communicated by circular, culminated a series of warnings to the courts from the Minister of Justice concerning the ticket system, quoted above. See the circulars of July 7, 1844 and December 14, 1859, in the Ministère de la justice, *Recueil officiel des instructions et circulaires* 2: 72, 480; October 21, 1887, in the Ministère de la justice, *Bulletin . . . , année 1886*, 224–226; February 1, 1891, in the *Bulletin . . . , année 1891*, 3–4. The view of republican legislators in 1870 and during the Third Republic was that privileged access to the courtroom was a violation of free publicity, newly reconciling judicial and republican rationales. On criticism in the legislature of the reserved seating

at the Troppmann trial, see Drachline, 185, 190–191.

61. For comment on the press box, see Sorel, 1078 (including the complaint about the partition between the press and jury boxes); L.-J. Faverie, "Les nouvelles salles d'assises au Palais de Justice," *Gazette des tribunaux* (October 30, 1868): 1036. Special boxes for the press appear, however, to have been instituted in Paris penal courtrooms at least by the mid 1840s (see fig. 34, showing the old criminal courtroom circa 1846); Pierre Jacomet, *Le Palais sous la Restauration, 1815–1830*, 2nd ed. (Paris: Plon-Nourrit, 1922), 9, says they did not exist during the Restoration. On the press at Troppmann's trial: Petit-Jean, "Courrier du Palais," *Le Monde illustré* (January 1, 1870): 11 (where the claim of 20,000 readers is made); *Gazette des tribunaux* (December 29, 1869); *Petit journal* (December 25, 1869): 2 (the claim of the press to monopolize publicity), (December 29, 1869): 1 (regarding the human wreath), (January 1, 1870): 1; *Le Crime de Pantin, édition complète illustrée* (Paris, n.d.), 94. (The latter is available at the Bibliothèque historique de la ville de Paris, call number 9598.) For a description of the organization of the courtroom as of December 1959, after the jury box had been filled by the press, see Sybille Bedford, *The Faces of Justice: A Traveller's Report* (New York: Simon and Schuster, 1961), 284. The press migrated more than once, however: as of 1892, it had been transferred across the courtroom to the defendant's dock, where it was segregated from the accused by a movable partition: Presse judiciaire, 276.

62. On the significance of noise and corporate introduction, see Garapon, 51–52; on the symbolism of red robes, Garapon, 70. See also Du Camp, 3: 175: "Cela est d'une majesté vraiment imposante." According to Marcel Rousselet, *Histoire de la magistrature française des origines à nos jours*, 2 vols. (Paris: Plon, 1957), 1: 335, this spectacle of shared red robes was relatively new to Paris, where it had only been instituted at the beginning of the Second Empire.

63. On the significance of the chief prosecutor's presence, see Bérard, 1: 253–254; Martinage, 147. On the French origins of the public prosecutor, see Esmein, 114ff.; on the responsibilities of the prosecutor vs. the examining judge, see Garraud in Esmein, 42–44, and Esmein, 500ff. Garner, 255–256, particularly noted the prosecutor's power to supervise and intervene in the careers of examining judges.

64. Du Camp, *Revue des deux mondes* 82 (August 15, 1869): 852–853, reprinted in his book, *Paris*, 3: 151–153; L.-A. Prévost-Paradol, *La France nouvelle*, 2nd ed. (Paris: Michel Lévy, 1868), chap. 3, esp. 158–162. However, Prévost-Paradol refrained from spelling out what was common knowledge at the time, and would explode in critiques published in the early Third Republic: that tenure was itself a tenuous affair. With each new political upheaval, the magistrature was purged, often by being required to swear an oath of allegiance to the new ruler, whose constitution or charter specified a revised basis for sovereignty and/or the source of justice. Thus when the Bourbon Restoration fell in the Revolution of 1830, the Paris bar suspended work, declaring that it could not plead until it knew in whose name judgments would now be made. For accounts of judicial tenure and purges published in the 1870s, see Odilon Barrot, *De l'organisation judiciaire en France* (Paris: Didier, 1872); Jules Favre, *De la réforme judiciaire* (Paris: Plon, 1877). More recent historical accounts include Marcel Rousselet, *La Magistrature sous la Monarchie de Juillet* (Paris: Sirey, 1937), 23, 46–49; Jean-Pierre Royer, *La Société judiciaire depuis le XVIIIe siècle* (Paris: PUF, 1979), 304–316; Jean-Louis Debré, *La Justice au XIXe siècle. Les magistrats* (Paris: Perrin, 1981), 47–62. The Association française pour l'histoire de la

justice in Paris currently is planning a conference on judicial purges.

65. The quotation is from *Le Petit journal* (December 28, 1869): 1. On the selection of the president and his two colleagues and their relationship to the prosecution, see Cruppi, 109–114. The role and powers of the president are laid out by Nouguier, passim, esp. 3: 550–567, 615–617. Nouguier, 3: 162, warned that the president may be suspected of taking sides; Cruppi said outright, 39–40: "Président et accusateur ont tous deux le même costume, et, de rouge vêtus, familiers et échangeant des signes, ils sont assis dans deux fauteuils semblables. . . . Ce voisinage intime des conseillers et du ministère public, cette alliance créée par la fonction et l'uniforme, par les moeurs et les traditions, fortifient les soupçons de notre juré à l'égard des deux magistratures." For more recent commentary on the relationship of the prosecutor to the judge as opposed to the defense counsel in the context of comparative analysis of courtroom ritual and furnishings, see Bedford; John Hazard, "Furniture Arrangement as a Symbol of Judicial Roles," *Etc.: A Review of General Semantics* 19, no. 2 (July 1962): 181–188; also see Martin, *Crime*, 177, 178. For a Second Empire interpretation of rank as implied by furniture, see Rigaud, 298: "Les témoins sont tout à fait mal traités; . . . on leur offre des bancs de bois. . . . La Cour, au contraire, a des sièges excellents, soigneusement rembourrés, admirablement arrondis. . . . Les jurés, par exemple, n'ont que des chaises; il faut conserver les distances et maintenir les traditions. . . . Les avocats gardent leur banc, fort modeste et fort humble, mais ils sont fiers, parce qu'ils l'illustrent." See Royer and Debré for a general sociological analysis of the esprit de corps in the magistrature, the professional ethos of reserve (esp. Royer, 287–303, although Royer stresses its political utility without acknowledging its basis in a tradition of mag-

isterial authority), and differences between the magistrature and the bar (esp. the 1865 comment of Pinard, then a judge, quoted in Royer, 266–267).

66. "[I]ntelligents, moraux, amis de l'ordre et de la loi," according to G. Rousset, "De la correctionnalisation des crimes," *Revue critique de législation* (1855): 257, quoted by Luc Passion, "La politique du Second Empire en matière de criminalité: l'exemple de Paris," *Bulletin de la Société d'histoire moderne*, series 16, no. 11, 80th year (1981): 12–21, esp. 14.

67. On changes in jury selection and procedure and their rationales, as well as evidence of Second Empire surveillance of jurors, see Schnapper, 184–185, 194, 206–207. For a summary of the jury requirements and selection procedure contemporary with Troppmann's trial, see the jurors' handbook of 1867 by the Paris appellate judge Berriat, *Le Jury*, 15–32, 38–44. Berriat differs from Schnapper in stating that property was not a requirement (16), as Schnapper says it had become in 1850 (200). Ambroise Buchère, "Etude historique sur les origines du jury," *Revue historique de droit français et étranger* 8 (1862): 145–202, offers a Second Empire prosecutor's justification of the 1853 law (198–201), amplifying Schnapper's conclusions from legislative documents. For a social profile of Paris jurors in the late 1860s, see Schnapper, 235. According to Cruppi, 18–29, the jury make-up as of 1895 was quite similar, notwithstanding a change of jury law in 1872; however, Schnapper's analysis suggests that by the late 19th century the proportion of independently wealthy declined while that of petty bourgeois increased. The exemption for workers was only dropped in 1908, finally broadening the class base of the jury; women were only added in 1944, when they gained the vote.

68. Although tougher than their provincial counterparts, Parisian juries awarded ex-

tenuating circumstances in a rising percentage of cases during the Empire; while the rate during the July Monarchy decade of 1835–45 had been only 51%, the rate during the 1850s averaged 59% and rose to 68% for the decade of the 1860s. This is what prompted the complaints of the Ministers of Justice Delangle and Ollivier, in their statistical reports on penal justice for 1860 and 1868, respectively. Passion, "La politique," esp. 17; Ministère de la justice, *Compte-général de l'administration de la justice criminelle* (Paris: Imprimerie impériale), report on 1860 and the preceding decade, published 1862, 39; report on 1868, published 1870, ix-xvii. On liberal demand for jury reform, see Schnapper, 208–209. However, Schnapper, 208, comes to the opposite conclusion about the behavior of Second Empire juries; this discrepancy is probably due to the fact that Schnapper considered only acquittal rates, whereas a key statistic, from the point of view of 19th-century jurists, was the rate of extenuating circumstances—as Passion's interpretation acknowledges. James Donovan's significant article on jury prejudices, "Justice Unblind: The Juries and the Criminal Classes in France, 1825–1914," *Journal of Social History* 15 (Autumn 1981), 89–107, similarly does not consider extenuating circumstances. For commentary on the role of extenuating circumstances, see the second part of this essay.

69. Cf. Cruppi, 29–36, who indicates that in his day, session jurors assembled in their own deliberation chamber to await a call to descend to the magistrates' deliberation chamber, where a specific jury for the trial would be chosen; only after this formality did jurors enter the courtroom. I have instead followed the sequence of events described in newspaper accounts of Troppmann's trial, which effectively dramatize the emergence of the jury from the public, and which generally make much of the sequence

of formalities and the sense of time that they generated in the courtroom. While they manipulate sequence somewhat to suit their stories, *Le Petit journal* and the *Gazette des tribunaux* accounts agree on the steps by which the Troppmann jury was installed.

70. Cruppi, 37–41; Bérard, 1: 26–27. The jury rooms are described in reviews of the Cour d'assises at its inauguration, including Rigaud, 298; Faverie, 1036.

71. On the change in the relationship between the jury and the bench, see Merle and Vitu, 2: 730–32; Bedford, 224. On the relationship between the jury and the prosecutor: Du Camp, 3: 181; Berriat, *Le Jury*, 68.

72. Nouguier, 3: 67, 72, instructed the president on how to invest this ritual with the necessary solemnity. The *Gazette des tribunaux* commented (December 29, 1869): "Cette formalité emprunte à la gravité exceptionnelle de cette affaire un caractère encore plus important de solennité et de grandeur." Similarly, Nouguier, 3: 469, wrote of the oaths for witnesses: "[I]l élève la fonction du témoin jusqu'à une sorte de fonction publique." As noted above, legislative debate on the Second Empire's jury law of 1853 articulated what was implicit in the ritual—that the juror should conceive of himself as *fonctionnaire*.

73. Davis, *Fiction*, 38 and note 13, 171. However Berriat, *Le Jury*, 127, advised jurors: "Mais dans l'usage, les jurés ne se prévalent pas de ce droit; faute d'un costume uniforme [the very badge of their lay status!], il pourrait resulter de la diversité des coiffures, des bigarrures contraires à la dignité de l'audience."

74. My translation; I have retained the French term *intime conviction* because its meaning was a matter of debate among the French, but it has been translated as "Are you thoroughly convinced?" in the English edition of Esmein, 516. The French text is as follows: "La loi ne demande pas compte aux jurés des moyens par lesquels ils se sont

convaincus; elle ne leur prescrit point de rè-
gles, desquelles ils doivent faire particulière-
ment dépendre la plénitude et la suffisance
d'une preuve; elle leur prescrit de s'interroger eux-mêmes dans le silence et le re-
cueillement, et de chercher, dans la sincérité
de leur conscience, quelle impression ont
faite sur leur raison les preuves rapportées
contre l'accusé, et les moyens de sa défense.
La loi ne leur dit point: *Vous tiendrez pour
vrai tel fait attesté par tel ou tel nombre de
témoins;* elle ne leur dit pas non plus: *Vous ne
regardez pas comme suffisamment établie toute
preuve qui ne sera pas formée de tel procès-
verbal, de telles pièces, de tant de témoins ou de
tant d'indices;* elle ne leur fait que cette seule
question qui renferme toute la mesure de
leurs devoirs: *Avez-vous une intime conviction?"*

75. Nouguier 3: 508–509: "*L'oralité* du
débat est donc la règle fondamentale, absolue, et j'ajoute: la règle nécessaire. Sans elle,
l'institution du jury serait faussée, dans son
principe, et impossible, dans son application. Pour le jury, l'entrée du témoin, sa
physionomie, son attitude, son accent sont
autant d'éléments de confiance ou de dis-
crédit. Un mot, un geste, un regard, une
impression mal contenue, un embarras mal
dissimulé, un mouvement involontaire de
trouble ou d'indignation, tout peut servir,—
au milieu des interpellations qui s'échan-
gent, des contradictions dont le choc fait
jaillir la lumière,—à mettre à nu la pensée
secrète du témoin. Supprimez tout cela, ou
plutôt substituez à tout cela une froide analyse du dossier, une lecture plus froide en
core des pièces qui le composent ou des déclarations écrites qu'il renferme, et vous
enlevez au jury ces éléments moraux, ces
preuves vivantes, à l'aide desquelles, selon
son serment, s'éclaire sa *conscience* et se forme
son *intime conviction*."

The distinction between judges of law and
judges of fact is standard; see, for example,
Nouguier, 4: part 1, 59–60. On the difference between legal versus moral proofs, to
which it is related, see Esmein, 251–271,
434, 516, and the appendix by Garraud,
620–630.

76. Berr, 490.

77. If the juror's obligation to contem-
plate a tableau of visual and verbal evidence
silently, searching his heart for its meaning,
recalls the 18th-century prescription for audience response to the *drame bourgeois*, the
public's intervention in the drama and the
drama's own frequent lack of consistency
generated theatricality.

78. Historicizing Foucault's concept,
Goldstein, 86, 378–79, and Harris (more
loosely, in discussing suggestion as a tool of
popular healers and psychiatrists), 200, have
noted 19th-century recognition of the significance of the expert gaze in psychiatry. The
19th-century juxtaposition and attempted
reconciliations of the gaze of the expert and
that of the juror in the courtroom deserve
more exploration.

79. See the treatise by Julien Guadet sum-
marizing standard practice for major building types, *Eléments et théorie de l'architecture*,
4 vols., orig. pub. 1901–04, 5th ed. (Paris:
Librairie de la construction moderne, n.d.
[c. 1923]), 2: 482–484. Unilateral lighting
in penal courtrooms was probably an innovation established in the mid-century at the
Paris Palais, which then set the model for
provincial courthouse design. It is not seen
in exemplary courthouse projects from the
first third of the 19th century. The plans for
Abadie the elder's provincial courthouse in
Angoulême, of 1825, published as a model
by Gourlier, Biet, Grillon and Tardieu,
*Choix d'édifices publics projetés et construits en
France depuis le commencement du XIXe siècle*
(Paris: L. Colas, 1825–1850), show windows on both sides of the criminal court-
room, as do the plans by Louis-Pierre Baltard for Lyon, published in his *Projet du
Palais de Justice de la ville de Lyon* in 1830. As
Baltard was the theory professor at the

Ecole des beaux-arts and a member of the national architectural review board for public buildings, his work would have represented the most sophisticated formulation of the building type at that moment. As for the evidence from the Palais in Paris, the first project for rebuilding the criminal courts, by the equally sophisticated architect Jean-Nicolas Huyot, from 1835–1840, also intended windows on both sides, although an 1846 print of the old criminal courtroom which the new one replaced shows unilateral lighting (fig. 55). Duc's projects for the criminal courtrooms, from the earliest one of 1847, show unilateral lighting, as do the new misdemeanors courtrooms he designed and built at the Palais between 1844 and 1851. In Duc's misdemeanors courts, unilateral windows were not specified in the program but were necessitated by the exiguity of the site; however, they were clearly recognized as a virtue, for they were specified in the program established in 1848 for the criminal courts, where layout permitted windows on both sides (Archives nationales, F/21/1867, report of July 7, 1853 by Caristie to the Conseil général des bâtiments civils). Commentators on the new courtroom and its proceedings pointed out the lighting and its purpose, but did not perceive it as a new feature; for example, Du Camp, 3: 175.

80. For very specific instructions on jury demeanor and penalties for inappropriate behavior, see the jury manuals by Berriat, 128, and André Cambréal, *Le Jury criminel. Comment se forme, délibère et statue le jury de la Cour d'assises* (Paris: Rousseau, 1937), 39–40. Cambréal told jurors that they must guard against those involuntary gestures, like a shrug of the shoulders or a nod of the head, which they themselves watched for in the witnesses and defendant. Commentators tended to merely note the impassivity of the jury—"immobile comme un sphinx d'Egypte," in the words of Du Camp, 3:

183—and pass on to more expressive subjects.

Roger Allou and Charles Chenu, *Barreau de Paris. Grands avocats du siècle* (Paris: A. Pedone, 1894), 234, described how the defense lawyer Lachaud habitually exploited his disadvantageous situation on a bench below the defendant's box facing the light, to surreptitiously survey the jury: "Il était à demi renversé sur son banc, la tête légèrement inclinée sur l'épaule droite, mais ne perdant pas un instant de vue les douze jurés qu'il lui fallait conquérir, sans que ceux-ci eussent le soupçon de l'infatigable attention dont ils étaient l'objet. . . . Comme pour se protéger du jour trop vif qui frappe de face le visage de l'avocat placé à la barre de la Cour d'assises, Lachaud fronçait le sourcil ou plaçait la main au-dessus de ses yeux: mais c'était pour mieux apercevoir les impressions qui se peignaient sur les traits mobiles de ses juges." See also Pierre de la Gorce, "Le barreau sous le Second Empire," *La Revue de Paris* 40 (May 15, 1933): 255–256. In fact, journalists at Troppmann's trial—as in *Le Petit journal* (December 31, 1869), 2—noted Lachaud's posture, head in hands, with some puzzlement.

81. See, for instance, Berr, esp. 494–96, on the rarity with which jurors exercised their right to take notes or to pose questions.

82. While this view, showing Troppmann's confrontation with the evidence, including a model of the field at Pantin set before the jury, does not emphasize the dossier, documents and files are prominent in many courtroom scenes.

83. "The Paris of the Second Empire in Baudelaire," 46–47, and "Paris—the Capital of the 19th Century," 169, in Benjamin, *Charles Baudelaire: A Lyric Poet in the Era of High Capitalism*, trans. Harry Zohn (London: Verso Editions, 1983).

84. Both drawings are in the Manuscripts Department of the Bibliothèque nationale: *L'Envieux/Barkilphedro*, n.a.f. 13.352, fol.

24; *Judex*, n.a.f. 13.356, fol. 1. They belong to the group of four albums that have been interpreted as a collection of diverse caricatures assembled by Victor Hugo circa 1869 and entitled "Le Théâtre de la Gaîté," after a popular Parisian theater from the boulevard du crime—underlining the association between theater and justice. René Journet and Guy Robert, *Théâtre de la Gaîté* (Paris: Les Belles Lettres, 1961); Jean Massin, ed., *Victor Hugo, Oeuvres complètes, édition chronologique*, vol. 17: *Oeuvre graphique*, vol. 1 (Paris: Club français du livre, 1967), figs. 565 and 845, x-xi.

L'Envieux/Barkilphedro, a portrait of Barkilphedro in Hugo's novel *L'Homme qui rit*, is not strictly speaking a criminal under scrutiny—in fact, he exercises *"surveillance,"* in Hugo's words, being a spy both of people in high places and of jetsam. However, he is the type of the envious man (Hugo explained that such desire is the precondition for espionage, a crime of which Troppmann was also suspected), and Hugo characterized him similarly in text and image. Hugo's description in *L'Homme qui rit* was written between 1866–68; Journet and Robert have dated the drawing to the year after the novel's publication. *Judex*'s title is unambiguous, but its particular meaning or context for Hugo has not been analyzed. This judge is unusual among the caricatures of the four albums in being shown full-face rather than in Hugo's more standard profile. But there is no apparent pattern that would explain why a minority of Hugo's caricatures, including *Judex*, are frontal, and it must be said Hugo also caricatured judges in profile. It is not clear that Hugo explicitly meant to show *Judex* from the vantage point of the public in the courtroom. Yet it is striking that Paul Savey-Casard selected just this frontal judge and profiled miscreant to illustrate his study of Hugo's views on crime, *Le Crime et la peine dans l'oeuvre de Victor Hugo* (Paris: PUF, 1956), given that jurist's familiarity with the courtroom and its vantage points. Hugo shared that familiarity, having been a habitué of the old criminal courtroom in Paris before his exile. On this, see Pierre Jacomet, *Le Palais sous la monarchie de juillet, 1830–1848* (Paris: Plon, 1927), 216.

85. Of course, eye-witness accounts disagreed on some important features, underlining the interdependence of what was noticed and noted with assumptions and interpretations. For instance, most commentators discussed whether or not Troppmann was shaven; some claimed he was clean-shaven so as to enhance his youthfulness, while others saw his stubble as a sinister shadow belying his bland features. Attention went to Troppmann's hand partly because tradition associated family murder with the hand that did the deed: until the reform of the penal code in 1832, parricide required not only decapitation by guillotine but also amputation of the right hand. Indeed, Troppmann was being touted as a successor to the famous murderer Lacenaire of the July Monarchy, whose large hand had been embalmed after his execution (even though Lacenaire was not a parricide and his execution postdated the reform) and could be seen at Du Camp's. On Du Camp's relic, see Savey-Casard, 12. For other perspectives on Troppmann's hand, see Perrot, 31–32. For descriptions of Troppmann, I have relied on *Le Petit journal*, the *Gazette des tribunaux*, and the *Crime du Pantin* published after the trial, based on "tous les renseignements publiés par la Presse au jour le jour," notably the *Figaro* and *Le Droit*. Petit-Jean, "Courrier du Palais," *Le Monde illustré* (January 1, 1870): 11, constructed his examination of Troppmann explicitly as a comparison to photographs.

On the physiognomic tradition, its importance in 19th-century popular and high culture, and its significance as a widely-shared "hermeneutic paradigm" (Sekula's term) for interpreting features and gestures, see Judith Wechsler, *A Human Comedy: Physiognomy and Caricature in Nineteenth-Century Paris* (Chicago: University of Chicago Press, 1982), and Alan Sekula, "The Body and the Archive," *October* 39 (Winter 1986), 3–64, esp. 10–14. For the legacy of this tradition in professional criminology towards the end of the century, specifically the mixed French reaction to the Italian school's doctrine of visibly stigmatized "born criminals," see in addition to Sekula, Robert Nye, *Crime*, chap. 4; Harris, 81–90. Harris notes that, notwithstanding the French preference for a sociological over a biological explanation of crime, the press dwelt on visual characteristics (131), and forensic psychiatrists were prone to base diagnoses of defendants partly on visual analysis of physical features supposed to indicate a pathological state (153–154); one should go further to link these discourses to the physiognomic tradition of interpreting types in an expanding and seemingly illegible mass society, for the expert was speaking to a jury that was officially charged with scrutinizing features and gestures—whether spiritualist or quasi-materialist in its interpretive frame. However, it is also necessary to take account of how this hermeneutic paradigm may have been affected by the work of the celebrated criminal photographer, Alphonse Bertillon, whose laboratory for documenting and identifying detainees was installed in 1888 in the voluminous attic directly above the criminal courtrooms in Paris. (The date is given in the prefect's report of October 27, 1888, to the Conseil général: Département de la Seine, *Procès-verbaux du Conseil général (1838–1938)* (Paris: various dates); this publication is available at the Bibliothèque administrative in the Hôtel de Ville, Paris.) Sekula argues that Bertillon developed an indexical rather than symbolic approach to the features of the defendant, fragmenting his or her body into isolated signs of individual identity, rather than assimilating individual bodily features into types. This would seem to be one endpoint for the movement in the criminal courts towards what the jurist Saleilles called in 1898 the individualization of judgment, or *l'individualisation de la peine*, and it suggests how an ideology of increasing attention to the individual effectively evaded the individuality of the defendant. Yet it is not clear to what extent juries, judges, and experts abandoned more traditional attributions of meaning to signs in carrying out the requisite psychological analysis of the defendant and the assessment of the threat he or she posed to society, especially in the context of the doctrine of solidarism.

Concerning the reliance of the physiognomic tradition on the profile view, see the key work by Johann Caspar Lavater, *Essays on Physiognomy designed to promote the knowledge and the love of mankind*, 5 vols., trans. from the French by Henry Hunter (London, 1792), esp. "Fragment Eleventh: Of Silhouettes," 2: 176–238. Lavater wrote repeatedly of the superior telling power of the profile: "The Physiognomist will dwell upon it in preference" (1: 261); "It is enough for me to have seen the angle formed by the jawbone from the ear to the chin, to discover a mind acute, profound and enterprising" (1: 259); "Silhouettes alone have extended my physiognomical knowledge, more than any other kind of portrait" (2: 177). As for the forehead, he confessed: "I was almost tempted to write a whole volume on the *forehead* only" (5: 273). This focus was perpetuated in the mug shot genre of the police photographer, which systematically incorporates profile views. On this, also see Druick (cited below), 237 and note 4. Thanks to the congruence between analytic paradigms and the physical point of view of the courtroom audience, artists in the courtroom typically sketched the defendant in profile, concentrating on symbolically loaded features like the forehead. Court artists favored profile views for the vignettes that filled popular magazines like the *Monde illustré*. Based on sketches made in the Paris courtroom at a trial in 1880, Edgar Degas similarly characterized two defendants in telling profile in the *Physiognomies de criminels* that he exhibited in the Impressionist show of 1881; see Douglas Druick, "La petite danseuse et les criminels: Degas moraliste?," in the Musée d'Orsay & Ecole du Louvre, *Degas inédit. Actes du Colloque Degas* (Paris: La documentation française, 1989), 224–250, esp. 236–237.

86. Nouguier, 3: 90: "C'est à ce moment que les jurés reçoivent la première révélation des faits; que, préparés ainsi à l'étude de l'affaire, il la commencent par l'étude de l'homme, en suivant ses impressions, ses attitudes, ses mouvements et en cherchant à pressentir, à l'aide de ces premières données, les secrets sentiments de son âme." As for the defense, it had received copies of these documents at least five days before the trial (87).

87. Both sides were informed of the witnesses to be called by the other shortly before the trial, with the intention of avoiding surprise tactics. Even the order of the witnesses, an element of drama and skill which shapes a case in an American trial, was established ahead of time, and by the prosecutor. Nouguier, 3: 275–276, 463–464; John E. Simonett, "The Trial as One of the Performing Arts," *American Bar Association Journal* 52 (December 1966): 1145.

88. Nouguier, 3: 137–163: "[The interrogation] est un des moyens les plus efficaces d'engager, dès début, le débat contradictoire, par la mise en contact du système de l'accusation et de celui de la défense. En mettant ainsi en relief les concessions faites et les points contestés, on a le grand avantage de circonscrire, d'avance, le champ réservé aux investigations de l'audience, de noter, en quelque sorte, chacune des difficultés à résoudre, chacune des preuves dont le ministère public et l'accusé comptent tirer parti, de préparer, en un mot, les esprits à l'étude et à l'intelligence de détails plus ou moins nombreux, détails graves, pour les uns, secondaires, pour les autres, et dont une ligne de démarcation bien tranchée vient de déterminer la véritable importance" (142–143).

89. It is telling that Berriat, in his juror's manual of 1867, 73, felt obliged to defend the interrogation at length, lest jurors suspect its motives. On the general problem, Barrot noted, 120–121: "La violence déployée à l'audience contre l'accusé provoque presque infailliblement une réaction en sa faveur dans les délibérations du jury, et ainsi ce zèle déployé pour mieux assurer la vindicte publique se retourne presque toujours contre elle." On the systemic nature of this problem, 121: "[C]'est parce que les présidents des assises sont spécialement chargés d'interroger les accusés et les témoins qu'ils sont entraînés à se faire accusateurs. C'est le législateur lui-même qui les a placés sur cette pente où il leur est bien difficile de ne pas glisser."

90. Garapon, 93–97, 101, interprets the interrogation as a sacrificial rite in which the defendant is forcibly delivered to society (to restore its purity and unity) by virtue of the fact that he must participate in a ritual whose rules are generally unfamiliar to him, but second nature to the president. For a reconstruction of the defendant's experience of interrogation in the Paris criminal courts of the 1870s, see Joëlle Guillais, *Crimes of Passion, Dramas of Private Life in Nineteenth-Century France*, orig. pub. Paris, 1986, trans. Jane Dunnett (Cambridge: Polity Press, 1990), esp. 218–228. Guillais analyzes a series of cases as a historical record of working-class life experience, whose account was systematically repressed in the courtroom.

91. On surprise tactics, see Bérard, 1: 210–216. Defendants resorted increasingly

to this tactic over the course of the century, apparently gaining confidence in confronting expert interrogation. Bérard's late 19th-century experience led him to conclude that a president could no longer maintain the systematic deductive approach: "[L]'argumentation progressive, qui est cependant dans la logique, ne valait plus rien; . . . dans la lutte moderne pour la verité, il ne fallait plus garder le meilleur argument pour la fin, mais ouvrir le feu tout de suite . . . "

92. For a president's perspective on the tendencies of defendants to resist self-revelation, yet to incriminate themselves, see Bérard, 1:39–43, 162–165. More generally, Nouguier, 3: 143–144, explains how obliging the defendant to respond actively to the charges enables the jury to appraise his moral performance.

93. For instance, opponents of the prison system isolating detainees in single cells, a system pioneered in the United States and partially introduced in France, claimed that the inherently sociable French could not tolerate the deprivation of conversation. Gordon Wright, *Between the Guillotine and Liberty: Two Centuries of the Crime Problem in France* (Oxford & New York: Oxford University Press, 1983), 75.

94. From *Le Crime de Pantin*: Troppmann: "Pourquoi n'a-t-on pas fait des recherches sur ce que je disais?" (114); President: "Comment esperez-vous que la justice et le jury vous croient . . . ; qui peut, en présence de tant de déclarations différentes, croire à votre dernière version de complices mystérieux?" (112); Pres.: "Vous mentiez donc?" T: "Oui, monsieur" (101); T: "Croyez-vous que tous ces enfants seraient restés là pour se laisser tuer?" Pres.: "Je n'entre pas dans vos hypothèses; je vous rappelle ce que vous avez dit vous-même" (112). Relative to other trials of the period, the president's tone was but moderately partisan: "Vous vouliez devenir riche à tout

prix (116); "Jamais préméditation plus odieuse n'a été mieux établie!" (108).

In an exchange recounted by the *Gazette des tribunaux* (December 29, 1869), the president asked Troppmann to recount his murders of Madame Kinck and her children, which Troppmann did because it was the only way he could specify the roles of his alleged accomplices. The effect was sensationally incriminating, and guided the reporter in reading savagery into an ambiguous demeanor elsewhere reported as mild, calm, modest, and accompanied by childish diction: "Ce recit, pendant lequel le public retient sa respiration, est difficilement entendu à raison de la prononciation défectueuse de l'accusé [due to his German accent] et du ton peu élévé de sa voix. Il l'a fait pourtant d'un ton assuré, tournant presque le dos au public et fixant les yeux vers le bas du bureau de la Cour. Ses deux longues mains sont appuyées sur la balustrade; nous l'apercevons seulement de profil. Sa tête est presque rejetée en arrière, et son attitude est d'une fermeté sauvage et presque provocante."

95. Cruppi, 82.

96. *La nouvelle peinture. À propos du groupe d'artistes qui expose dans les galeries Durand-Ruel*, orig. pub. 1876, reprint ed., ed. by Marcel Guerin (Paris: Floury, 1946), 42: "Avec un dos, nous voulons que se révèle un tempérament, un âge, un état social; par une paire de mains, nous devons exprimer un magistrat ou un commerçant; par un geste, toute une suite de sentiments." This celebrated passage continues, prescribing for artists and viewers of art, the work of a juror: "La physionomie nous dira qu'à coup sûr celui-ci est un homme rangé, sec et méticuleux, et que celui-là est l'insouciance et le désordre même. L'attitude nous apprendra que ce personnage va à un rendez-vous d'affaires, et que cet autre revient d'un rendez-vous d'amour. *Un homme ouvre une porte, il*

entre, cela suffit: on voit qu'il a perdu sa fille." These words referred specifically to the work of Degas, who in fact submitted some pastels based on sketches made at the Paris Cour d'assises to the Impressionist show of 1881; see Druick, "La petite danseuse."

97. This is perhaps a modest instance of the kind of skill-matching that Michael Baxandall described in *Art and Experience in Fifteenth-Century Italy: A Primer in the Social History of Pictorial Style* (Oxford: Oxford University Press, 1972), concerning the gauging abilities of merchant-patrons. The reciprocity of drawing personality and interpreting it had marked the physiognomic tradition since Lavater, who advised his readers as though they were both portrait artists and readers of physiognomy.

This observation on genres of trial illustration is based on *Le Monde illustré*, where the vignettes began to give way to cropped views of a given section of the courtroom and its users, simulating photographs, during the first decade of the 20th century. Although such vignettes are hardly limited to trial illustration, the form so closely meets the demands of trials that it would be interesting to pursue the significance of trial illustration and judgment in the larger history of the genre.

98. On the validity of character witnesses, see Nouguier, 3: 536. The French system of testimony replaces the Anglo-American one of cross-examination. After speaking freely, witnesses could be questioned directly by the judges, jurors, or the prosecutor—all construed as impartial figures in the trial— or indirectly, through the agency of the president, by the accused, the defense counsel, or the *partie civile*, all interested parties whose words need mediation by an impartial judge. In practice, the president tended to ask many questions (Cruppi, 82), while other parties were restrained. The order of witnesses was established by the prosecutor,

and normally began with those for the prosecution: Nouguier, 3: 240–614.

99. *Le Petit journal* (December 31, 1869), 1, 2.

100. For example, the *Gazette des tribunaux* (December 31, 1869): "C'est un jeune homme vigoreux, assez grand, bien pris, au visage mâle, au teint bronze, à la barbe noire . . . " The salvation scene is commemorated in the vignette at the left in fig. 27. Cruppi, 84–86, articulated a widespread late-century complaint about the jury's ability to appraise witness testimony when he wrote that jurors were insufficiently critical of the content and too easily seized by impressions of form and style. Of course, form and style were officially defined as a legitimate part of their evidence, and as Ong has pointed out in commenting on the mnemonic aspects of oral style, one of the reasons why that came easily to them was that style made a given witness memorable, within the stream of sixty-nine often fragmentary testimonies. This condition encouraged the staging of dramatic confrontations, sometimes even contained within the presentation of a single witness. For instance, the coachman who had driven the Kinck mother and children from Paris to the field where they were killed made a tremendous impression by mimicking Troppmann's voice in recounting Troppmann's treacherous conversation with the children, dramatizing evil and innocence in tone of voice and distinguishing his own voice, in a trial full of reflections on the alien voices of Alsatians in general. The *Gazette des tribunaux* noted (December 30, 1869): "A ces mots, que le cocher Bardot prononce en adoucissant sa grosse voix, comme pour imiter le ton dont Troppmann s'est servi, un long frémissement court dans l'auditoire."

101. *Le Crime de Pantin*, 167; *Gazette des tribunaux* (December 30, 1869): "Je ne suis pas taillé en Hercule, vous le voyez bien."

Only once did the *Gazette des tribunaux* detect real passion in Troppmann's responses, and even then it hesitated over the right interpretation: "Troppmann en ce moment, au lieu de saisir et de serrer de ses deux mains la balustrade des accusés, ce qui constitue sa gesticulation ordinaire, projette la main droite en avant. . . . La vivacité de Troppmann a un caractère tout particulier et difficilement définissable. C'est une vivacité de paroles qui n'ôte rien à sa figure de sa placidité ordinaire. Est-ce l'éclat soudain d'une violence concentrée? est-ce un simple calcul?" (December 30, 1869).

102. Berriat, *Le Jury*, 94–95.

103. President Thévenin declared during the testimony: "Voyons, Troppmann, . . . qu'il y ait chez vous l'ombre d'un sentiment de repentir que je n'ai pas encore trouvé." *Le Crime de Pantin*, 125.

104. *Gazette des tribunaux* (December 31, 1869); *Le Crime du Pantin*, 167, 173–75.

105. Bérard, 2: 147–148: "Le rôle du médecin légiste qui expose devant les jurés le résultat de ses contestations est très complexe; il faut qu'il fasse des leçons, sans en donner, car les jurés doivent apprendre par lui ce qu'ils ignorent, mais ils se cabreraient s'ils apercevaient une velléité de leur dicter une opinion; il faut cependant de l'autorité dans la parole, car si le médecin doute, qui croira? Il faut, tout en restant l'homme de l'art, inspirer la pitié pour les souffrances d'autrui et savoir émouvoir . . . "

106. Nouguier, 3: 724, 727–729.

107. Nouguier, 3: 724: "J'aurais montré le procureur général se levant sous cette impression qu'il doit compte à la société du coupable qu'il laisse impuni, et à Dieu de l'innocent qu'il fait condamner; —se souvenant qu'il a été institué pour poursuivre, non un succès de vanité, mais une satisfaction de conscience . . . , et que, pour atteindre ce but, il doit chercher, non à surprendre, mais à guider, non à éblouir, mais à éclairer, non à passioner, mais à convaincre. Je l'aurais applaudi, si ses paroles avaient été les interprètes fidèles de ses convictions, parce que la justice n'a pas de parti-pris; —si elles avaient été humaines, parce qu'il n'est le ministre que de la justice des hommes; —modérées, parce que la justice est sans haine; —calmes, parce qu'elle est sans colère; —mâles, parce qu'elle est, dans tous les états bien organisés, une des puissances viriles; —austères, parce que chacune d'elles est comme un écho de la morale et de la loi." Nouguier, 3: 729: "[D]ans le développement oral de l'accusation, le procureur général jouit d'une latitude absolue. . . . [P]ar cela seul qu'il n'a d'autre modérateur que lui-même, il lui est permis moins qu'à tout autre de manquer le modération." Also see Du Camp, 3: 181–182; Pinard, 56–57; Presse judiciaire, 391, which articulated "l'idéalisme représenté par l'avocat général," noting how the prosecutor "invoque les grands principes, parle au nom de la justice, de la famille, de la propriété."

108. Presse judiciaire, 391–393. Although that passage specifically describes a shift in pleading style among criminal lawyers during the Third Republic, after Troppmann's trial, it also emphasizes the longstanding tradition of the "émouvante plaidoirie" and its appeal through specificity of content. On provoking the prosecutor, see de la Gorce, 256.

109. Nouguier, 3: 724–725. "[P]our l'avocat, le devoir de conscience s'individualise. En lutte, dans l'intérêt d'un seul, contre l'intérêt de tous, il s'y dévoue, heureux, s'il fait acquitter un innocent, et sans remords, s'il fait acquitter un coupable. Organe de la défense d'autrui, il n'a pas à soumettre ce qu'il va dire au contrôle de sa propre conviction, parce que, lorsqu'il parle, c'est son client qui parle. A lui, . . . tous les accents et tous les tons. . . . le raisonnement et la loqique, le rire ou les larmes, le mouvement et la flamme. Qu'il éblouisse, et un

rayon des vives clartés de son éloquence se reflétera sur celui qu'il défend. Que, par l'ironie et le sarcasme, il excite le rire, et le juge se dira, peut-être, avec le poëte: *j'ai ri, me voilà désarmé.* Qu'il passionne son auditoire, pour exciter la pitié, et peut-être obtiendra-t-il de l'émotion des jurés un acquittement, qu'il aurait vainement demandé à leur raison. C'est là un des heureux privilèges de l'éloquence du barreau. Elle a devant elle un champ sans bornes et une liberté d'allures qui la distingue profondément, comme on le voit, de l'éloquence judiciaire." Similarly, Jacques Munier-Jolain, *La Plaidoirie dans la langue française*, 3 vols., orig. pub. 1896 (Geneva: Slatkine Reprints, 1971), 3: 317, pointed out, through the celebrated example of Berryer, how 19th-century lawyers acted out, rather than narrated, their cases.

Compare the lawyers' perspective, in Allou and Chenu, 236–237, who justify why and how Troppmann's lawyer Lachaud made cases for defendants whom the public considered reprehensible: "[P]our qui veut sonder la profondeur des bas fonds où se déroulent certaines vies, il n'est pas de criminel si dépravé en qui l'analyse ne révèle les tristesses à côté des vices. Avant d'aborder l'audience, l'avocat a passé dans la cellule de [the prison of] Mazas de longs tête-à-tête avec le misérable. . . . Dans cette intimité douloureuse, loin de cet appareil de publicité qui redresse plus qu'il n'incline la tête du fanfaron du crime, il a provoqué les confidences, a suivi l'enfance abandonnée du coupable; il a amené au bord de cette paupière dès longtemps desséchée une larme qu'il a recueillie avec la piété du prêtre au chevet du mourant. . . . Ce ne sera plus entre les quatre murs de l'étroite cellule que le drame va se dérouler, mais dans la vaste enceinte de la Cour d'assises, devant ces jurés qui pour la première fois verront le criminel et seront disposés à le juger sur la mine, sur les récits du crime publiés par la presse, en face d'un magistrat que ses fonctions et le froid examen de la procédure ont armé d'une implacable sévérité. Réussira-t-il à faire jaillir l'étincelle dont il a aperçu la lueur? . . . Ses adversaires sont nombreux et il est seul. Le président, l'avocat général, les témoins: autant de forces conjurées contre lui. A ses premiers efforts des murmures hostiles répondent du fond de la salle. Et cependant la liberté, la vie sont en jeu d'un homme qui a mis en lui sa suprême espérance. Pour propager les sentiments dont la source est en son coeur, pour remonter le fatal courant, ce n'est pas assez de toute son âme, il lui faut toutes les ressources de son esprit." In this scenario, the entire courtroom and its audience stand for the social order, and the only ethical course for the lawyer is, with his wits, to take on this Goliath. Imbalance in the French judicial duel justifies more melodramatic tactics than in the more consistently accusatorial courtroom of the British—a point Cruppi emphasized, as noted above.

110. For example, the protest issued by Henri Moreau, *Le Ministère public et le barreau, leurs droits et leurs rapports* (Paris: Jacques Lecoffre, c. 1860); see particularly the introduction by the lawyer Berryer, celebrated for his political independence and personal rhetorical style. A larger picture of Second Empire penal policy is sketched in note 141.

111. As expressed in the phrase "effets de manche."

112. For a characteristic comment about the lawyer's inherent alienation from himself, see F. Brunetière, "Sur l'éloquence judiciaire," *Revue des deux mondes* 87 (May 1, 1888): 218.

113. Damien, 438.

114. "[I]l est des distinctions dans le luxe de la robe et les manières de la porter: le plus souvent la queue de la robe est relevée, parfois elle traîne . . . ; les toques . . . se déforment différemment sous le coup de pouce

du propriétaire. . . . Le magistrat n'est plus, comme jadis, un type fixe . . . ; il est multiple . . . , comme l'humanité même. Vous verrez déboucher de la porte du fond, tantôt un juge hirsute, la toque sur l'oreille, la toge débraillée, tantôt un gommeux poupard ou un élégant élégiatique." Presse judiciaire; quoted by Sophie Loubriat, "Robe judiciaire et justice enrobée: histoire d'un costume professionnel," Proceedings of the 1983 colloquium, "Vers une anthropologie du vêtement," *Ethnographie* 130 (1984): 227–236, esp. 230–231. Loubriat perceptively points out this impregnation of the robe with individuality and its value in highlighting individual pleading style, but describes it historically as a manifestation of increasing individualism in the 19th century, which ultimately wears out the corporate symbols of judicial activity, especially the robe which conceals the sincere individual body beneath it. For our purposes, it was a prime instance of the larger cultural development of an ethos of personal style, in which lawyers were particularly important, and which by extension affected and undermined the corporate ethos of magistrates. It should be stressed that personal style in the 19th century, while affected by the discourse of transparency and sincerity developed in the Enlightenment, did not entail the shedding of form so much as the attribution of personality to objects that encased or were marked by the user.

115. On threadbare robes, Damien, 297; on the bar's requirement that lawyers appear to disdain worldliness and fees, meant to guarantee their independence and moral integrity, see Damien, passim, esp. 263–264, 294, 321–323, 372–383.

116. *Le Petit journal* (December 28, 1869): 2.

117. *Le Crime de Pantin*, 185–186: "Il usait de tous les artifices pour laisser subsister dans la cause quelque ombre où il pût se réfugier; mais une lumière vengeresse s'at-

tachait à lui, ne lui laissait aucun repos, et le montre inexorablement, enchaîné aux cadavres de ses victimes." For Grandperret's concluding appeal to responsibility and eternal justice, 199. On Troppmann's duplicity, 191: "Il sait composer son visage, et, l'assassinat dans l'âme, affecter les traits d'un ami . . . "

118. Colleagues rated Lachaud the best criminal lawyer of his day: see Pierre de la Gorce's reminiscences in "Le barreau," 255–257; Presse judiciaire, 286, 288. Allou and Chenu, 243, note Lachaud's "habitude prise de chercher ses inspirations dans les révélations même de l'audience." Félix Sangnier, in his publication of the *Plaidoyers de Charles Lachaud*, 1: x, declared Lachaud "un orateur inimitable, car il . . . ne parlait jamais que sous l'inspiration du moment et sous le souffle de la passion qui l'animait." The *Gazette des tribunaux* (December 31, 1869) reported the public response: "Du fond de la salle partent de violents murmures et des protestations hostiles." Lachaud's exclamation, "J'accomplirai mon devoir jusqu'au bout" provoked "marques d'approbation. Le silence le plus complet se rétablit." Lachaud himself is reputed to have observed, "Je joue du jury comme Paganini joue du violon" (Damien, 449).

119. Bérard, 1: 274. Sangnier, *Plaidoyers de Charles Lachaud*, 1: viii, credited Lachaud with expanding public interest in the psychology of the lower-class criminal defendant, a project that Lachaud in fact shared with forensic psychiatric experts. Also note Sangnier, 1: v-vi, on the oral character of Lachaud's style: "Ce qu'on ne reproduira jamais [in reprinting texts], ce sont ces élans de coeur, qui impressionnaient tant l'auditoire; ce sont ces gestes passionnés qui accentuaient la pensée et aussi cette voix, pleine d'harmonie, tantôt énergetique et puissante, tantôt douce et caressante, qui toujours vous captivait . . . "

120. *Gazette des tribunaux* (December

31, 1869): "'Si vous voulez de l'émotion, si vous voulez des larmes, je pourrai vous donner ce spectacle. Oui, il pleurera, je n'aurai qu'à lui parler de sa mère. . .' Tout l'auditoire, ému par ces paroles, se tourne vers l'accusé. Dès que son défenseur a parlé de sa mère, nous voyons la physiognomie de Troppmann se colorer, ses lèvres semblent trembler et aux derniers mots de Maître Lachaud (nous ne pouvons savoir si en réalité il pleure), pour la première fois depuis l'ouverture des débats, il parait ému; il baisse la tête, l'incline plus bas encore et disparaît complètement derrière la balustrade des accusés. Cet incident produit une profonde sensation. Nous le répétons, voilà la première signe d'émotion feinte ou réelle, que nous surprenons sur la physiognomie de Troppmann. Tout à l'heure même, alors que Monsieur le Procureur général rapportait en termes saisissants les scènes horribles de Pantin, il était d'une immobilité complète. On eut dit une statue." *Le Petit journal* (January 1, 1870), p. 3: "Maître Lachaud prononce ces paroles en se tournant vers l'accusé. L'auditoire entier suspendu à ses lèvres, se lève comme poussé par un mouvement magnétique. Troppmann—Troppmann qui n'a pas bronché encore, qui a écouté avec un calme impassible le réquisitoire fait contre lui, Troppmann, au nom de sa mère, se trouble et de grosses larmes coulent de ses yeux. Il se met sa tête entre ses deux mains, se baisse, se baisse jusqu'à disparaître derrière la balustrade." Compare, however, the skeptical comments of Du Camp, 3: 183, published in serial form before Troppmann's trial: "Chose étrange si dans la plaidoirie le défenseur parle des premières années de son client, de l'époque de pureté où l'idée même du crime lui était inconnue, il est sans example que le coupable, fût-il trois fois meurtrier, ne laisse tomber la tête entre ses mains et n'éclate en larmes."

121. Lachaud actually tried to disarm his audience by acknowledging the current status of monomania: "I see the smiles that my argument provokes . . . but in defending a man's life, I can only speak what I believe" (*Le Crime de Pantin*, 211). For Lachaud, that issue of conscience was doubt about the prevailing doctrine of free will, a doctrine the Imperial government had upheld in repressing dissenting views among the medical profession in an incident the previous year. It is interesting that Lachaud's very introduction of monomania constituted a theatrical surprise: after insinuating that the medical experts in the trial had capitulated to the prosecution's desire for conclusions against Troppmann, Lachaud produced his own expert—something technically disallowed in the criminal courts, where experts were preselected by the president. He cited an *Etude médico-légale au sujet de Troppmann*, by a doctor Amédée Bertrand, diagnosing Troppmann as a monomaniac. Privately published on December 27 to coincide with the trial, copies were distributed to reporters and the jury. Lachaud himself, however, made only partial use of Bertrand's arguments, which actually updated the definition of the purported disease in physiological terms which would become important in the courts of the Third Republic (Nye, *Crime*, 261). But Lachaud's effect was negligible, to judge by the *Gazette des tribunaux* and even *Le Crime de Pantin*, which abridged his remarks on monomania. On the brief career of monomania and its social significance, see Goldstein, 152–196; on government intervention on behalf of the doctrine of free will, ibid., 355–358. On the redefinition of the problem of responsibility after monomania's demise, see Harris, 30–47.

122. The battle between styles of prosecutor and defense lawyer in the Second Empire trial dramatizes the problem that Jean Starobinski, among others, has discussed as central to modern public oratory: the difficulty of persuading an audience

whose referent is no longer the sovereign monarch or divine authority, but rather itself as sovereign subject, who must be addressed both as individual and as a member of a transcendent collective interest. See "La chaire, la tribune, le barreau," in Pierre Nora, ed., *Les Lieux de mémoire* (Paris: Gallimard, 1986), vol. 2, part 3, 425–485, for a history of pre- and post-Revolutionary French attitudes towards alternate means of persuasion in public speeches.

123. *Le Petit journal* (January 1, 1870): 3. One reviewer of the new criminal court at its inauguration observed that the long stair to the jury room would at least give the jury time to forget the president's résumé before it began deliberation: Rigaud, 298. On the abolition, see Bérard, 1: 217–22.

124. *Le Petit journal* (January 1, 1870): 3. Du Camp, 3: 185, attested to the moving effect of this rare instance of apparently unfeigned emotion, even when performed by a professional actor: "Un acteur populaire à Paris, où il jouait depuis plus de vingt ans sur un théâtre très à la mode, étant chef du jury, fut tellement troublé au moment de faire connaître le verdict, qu'il ne put jamais lire la déclaration." Important here was the fact that the foreman looked like an individual dressed in ordinary clothes, without the corporate identity afforded by the robe.

125. Berriat, *Le Jury*, 102–120. The president could send the jury back for further deliberation, if he judged its sequence of answers inconsistent; this was one of the reasons why the foreman did not deliver the verdict in Troppmann's presence. The jurors' desks are noted by Berriat, *Le Jury*, 108; B. de Renjarde, "Chronique," *Le Petit journal* (October 31, 1868): 3.

126. "En ce moment, la salle de la cour d'assises présente un aspect lugubre. Seul, le bureau de la cour est éclairé par trois lampes, recouvertes chacune d'un abat-jour qui projette la lumière par terre, en laissant le haut dans une sorte de pénombre; les becs de gaz des deux lustres ont perdu beaucoup de leur éclat et reproduisent que des lueurs ternes. Les ors du plafond paraissent rouges; les panneaux de chêne semblent noirs. . . . Le public est presque tout entier dans l'ombre, les bougies des sténographes sont éteintes. Troppmann, debout, flotte pour ainsi dire dans une demi-lueur." *Le Petit journal* (January 1, 1870): 3.

127. On the applause, *Gazette des tribunaux* (December 31, 1869); *Le Crime de Pantin*, 214. For the performative aspect of spoken verdicts, Garapon, 137. The sentence was sovereign because it could not be appealed but only quashed for procedural reasons by the Cour de cassation or pardoned by the emperor.

128. Blandine Barret-Kriegel, "Regicide and Parricide," in Foucault, ed., *I, Pierre Rivière*, 219–229, for documentation of the correlation between regicide and parricide. It is striking that the old penalty for parricide—amputation of the hand that did the deed—was effected in the reproduction of Troppmann's amputated hand for didactic display (fig. 24).

129. Sangnier, *Plaidoyers de Charles Lachaud*, 2: 256; Drachline, 25 (and Drachline maintains that thesis himself); Perrot, "Fait divers," 914. Some claimed that Troppmann was a more direct enemy of the Empire, part of a pro-German Alsatian plot, which, for diplomatic reasons, the government refused to recognize in court: Perrot, "L'Affaire Troppmann," 31, 34; Drachline, 193.

130. In 1868, for instance, the Paris criminal courts had given no death sentences: Du Camp, 3: 187. In 1861, the conservative Rennes judge Eugène Lambert wrote: "[P]endant plusieurs années la peine capitale ne fût plus guère que nominale; cette epée de Damoclès n'effraya plus personne" (62). The national annual rate for actual executions had fallen from about 264 in the late Napoleonic Empire, to 72 in the late Resto-

ration, to 28 in the July Monarchy following a liberal reform of the penal code and jury deliberation in 1832, and to between 18 and 19 during the Second Empire (based on national statistics cited by Du Camp, 3: 304–305 and Wright, 168).

131. With ominous reports of popular agitation in the streets edging the newspaper accounts of Troppmann's appeals to the Cour de cassation and for imperial pardon, and his impending execution, it was an open question whether that spectacle would turn the attending crowd for or against the government. On this, see the abolitionist account by Turgenev, "L'exécution de Troppmann," in Isaac Pavolovsky, *Souvenirs sur Tourgueneff* (Paris: Albert Savine, 1887), 255–304. Turgenev's memoir was engineered by Maxime Du Camp, also an abolitionist (3: 309–312).

It should be noted, though, that the problem of public executions paralleled in exacerbated form the problems that were attributed to the presence of the public at the trial. As the Minister of Justice wrote in a circular of 1838–1839, "La réunion d'une grande foule fait de l'exécution d'une peine une sorte de spectacle populaire qui, loin de répandre d'utiles enseignements, peut contribuer à la dépravation des moeurs." A parliamentary report of 1870, in the wake of Troppmann's execution, asserted the need to discourage "cette avide curiosité que appelle tant de spectateurs à rechercher la vue de la sanglante tragédie." Du Camp, 3: 409 (pièces justificatives). For most misdemeanors and crimes, the spectacle of the trial replaced the old spectacle of punishment, then removed from public view, but in the case of capital crimes, legislators still argued in 1870 that the public execution served to demonstrate the seriousness of the entire hierarchy of otherwise invisible penalties which it culminated.

132. Sangnier, *Plaidoyers de Charles Lachaud*, 2: 311–312. Lachaud alluded to the removal of executions from public view in other countries; England had done so just the previous year. In the event, Troppmann's execution sparked another abolition initiative by republican deputies in the Corps législatif, but one that again aborted: see Drachline, 188–89; Wright, 169–170; Du Camp, 3: 407–415.

133. On the reform of 1832, see Berriat, *Le Jury*, 135–140; Esmein, 531–532; Patricia Moulin, "Extenuating Circumstances," in Foucault, ed., *I, Pierre Rivière*, 212–218; Schnapper, 187–188; Martinage, 70–71. For statistics on juries' use of extenuating circumstances versus acquittals, and commentary on their significance, see the annual report of the Ministère de la justice, *Compte-général de l'administration de la justice criminelle*, esp. the report on 1860 and the previous decade, published 1862, 37–39; report on 1868, published 1870, ix. The association of the jury with lenience is a 19th-century generalization; historians have explored the limits of jury lenience, arguing that middle-class juries protected their class interests, by studying different jury responses to different types of offenses. See Donovan; Passion, "La politique"; Martinage, passim; Schnapper, passim.

134. Lambert argued that law stems from God, meaning that "les lois ne sont donc pas seulement des conventions que les hommes se sont faites pour régler leurs rapports, mais des formules générales qui reproduisent les lois morales et naturelles antérieures à toutes les conventions" (6–7); consequently, he defined justice as something owed to subjects in return for obedience, rather than a right grounded in popular sovereignty and administered through its representative institutions (8). Finally, Lambert explained that the judge must teach the public and the jury in particular the values that the law embodies, and how to apply them in daily life: "C'est lui . . . qui doit expliquer, avant d'en faire l'application, non comme une leçon ab-

straite et dogmatique, mais comme un enseignement pratique, le sens littéral de la loi, sa conformit intime avec le fait, surtout son sens philosophique et sa portée morale" (27); "Ce n'est pas seulement ce qui se fait en cour d'assises qui importe beaucoup, mais ce qui se dit par la bouche de ses magistrats; . . . c'est la moralité générale qui se dégage de toute discussion publique pour porter au loin dans la foule un enseignement et un exemple" (28); regarding the jury, "Cette immixtion de l'homme privé, du simple citoyen dans les obligations du juge, doit avoir sur les moeurs publiques une autre influence que le résultat même du concours des jurés à l'administration de la justice: — c'est un caractère nouveau imprimé à leur personnalité, à leurs préoccupations habituelles, à la direction ordinaire de leur esprit; —ils apportent bien souvent du dehors des idées incomplètes, des préjugés même sur les pouvoirs publics, sur l'action de la justice criminelle; mais sous une bonne direction, dans ce sacerdoce d'un jour, dans cette participation à une sorte de culte public de la conscience et de la loi, ils deviendront plus sévères pour le mal, plus fermes pour le bien" (31). Also see Schnapper, 201. Here one should keep in mind Ong's observation, cited earlier, that a text (such as the Napoleonic codes) gains authority partly because its authors are invisible and abstract for the reader, and cannot be judged together with the contents of their writings.

135. Schnapper, 190, cites the earliest statement of this type known to him, which set a tone for later versions: A. Mahul, *Tableau de la constitution politique de la monarchie française selon la Charte* (1830), 552: "Les jurés sont, il est vrai, spécialement juges souverains du fait qui leur est soumis, mais ils sont aussi les délégués de la société pour sa protection et sa défense. Sous ce point de vue, n'ont-ils pas mission de corriger les vices même de la loi par tous les tempéra-

ments possibles: C'est ainsi que le jury peut protéger le pays contre les erreurs du pouvoir législatif et rendre la tyrannie impossible. . . . C'est qu'on appelle l'omnipotence du jury et n'est-ce pas précisément le triomphe d'une institution si excellente qu'elle pourvoit à l'inévitable imperfection de toute loi humaine?"

This view gained strength over the course of the century. For instance, the republican lawyer and politician Jules Favre wrote in 1877, 97–98, that the jury was an important moderating force which contributed "la circonspection, l'indulgence et la modération" to judgments, for professional judges, regardless of their good faith, could not help but bring "un esprit de système qui se [plie] mal aux nécessités si variables de la vie sociale. . . . un roideur inflexible, qu'on suppose peu compatible avec les inspirations de l'équité." And despite his great suspicion of oral trials, Cruppi declared, "Le juge de profession . . . a besoin, pour juger sainement, de rester en contact avec la conscience générale, de ne pas perdre de vue cette notion moyenne et populaire de la moralité qui est l'apport du juré dans l'oeuvre commune" (250).

136. For a historical overview of juridical schools of thought on the right to punish and responsibility, see Wright, 109–128; on the shift in emphasis from crime to criminal, the resultant "individualization" of the penalty and the social purposes of this shift during the Third Republic, see Harris, 108–116; Nye, *Crime*, chaps. 4, 6, 7; on Third Republic defense of the jury as an agent of individualization of the penalty, see Schnapper, 225. Whereas Harris differentiates between the earlier tradition of equity in the interests of the individual and the Third Republic's doctrine of individualizing sentences in the interests of what was called "social defense" (115), this account, with its focus on courtroom proceedings, suggests that the tradition of close examination of the

defendant was extended, applied toward new purposes, and appropriated by a new type of expertise. It should be noted that Martinage, who documents these shifts in relation to verdicts, nonetheless takes a different view of Third Republic practice, interpreting it not as a period of change but of "immobilisme"; she attributes significant implementation of flexible sentencing to the period after 1950 (13).

137. Savey-Casard, 176.

138. The most influential was Raymond Saleilles, *L'Individualisation de la peine* (Paris: Alcan, 1898).

139. Cruppi, 289–307; Tarde, "La foule et le public," *Revue de Paris* 4 (1898): 287–306, 615–35; Barrows, 145, 147, 154, 171. But this championing of the individual expert tended to reinforce the expert's subject, the individual in the crowd.

140. The new wing for the Chambres correctionnelles will be discussed in Taylor, *Modernizing the Palais de Justice*. For comment on the *correctionalisation* or demotion of many criminal cases at the end of the century, see Cruppi, 3–15; also see note 141.

141. When Du Camp republished his 1869 article on the Cour d'assises in *Paris*, after the fall of the Empire, he made a point of this historical situation in his *avertissement* to volume 3.

No one has attempted a systematic history of the diffuse Second Empire penal policy, although the work of Luc Passion and René Lévy points in that direction: Passion, "La politique," and "Conjuncture et géographie"; Lévy, "Un aspect de la mutation de l'économie répressive au XIXe siècle: la loi de 1863 sur le flagrant délit," *Revue historique* 274 (July-September 1985): 43–77. Cf. the general impressionistic appraisal by Pierre Guiral, "Réflexions sur la justice du Second Empire," in *La France au XIXe siècle, études historiques. Mélanges offerts à Charles Hippolyte Pouthas*, série études, vol. 4 (Paris: Sorbonne, 1973): 109–118. Of the many dimensions of imperial policy, a sample can be noted here. On government repression of challenges to the free will doctrine in 1865 and 1868, and on the discreditation of monomania circa 1852, see Goldstein, 355–359, 189–195; for a Second Empire Assises president's dismissal of the monomania defense, see Lambert, 266–281. Punishment was toughened. The government abolished the single-cell prison regime, which hard-liners viewed as an expensive coddling of prisoners by misguided philanthropists, and claimed to reestablish fear of imprisonment as a deterrent to crime. It also eliminated the much-criticized forced-labor camps or *bagnes*, blamed for perpetuating a criminal underworld made familiar by Balzac in the character of Jacques Collin in *Splendeurs et misères des courtisanes* (1839–47), and by Hugo in the early life of Jean Valjean, in *Les Misérables* (1862); it addressed the problem of recidivism by banishing forced-labor convicts to overseas penal colonies (Wright, 92–95, 99–102; Lambert, 59–61). As for the penal courts, there were two major changes. The revised jury law of 1853, discussed earlier, was acknowledged as a means to make juries tougher (Berriat, *Le Jury*, 11). That law was complemented by the ostensible reform of the penal code in 1863 (opposed by republicans such as Favre and Ollivier), which increased the powers of the police at the expense of the magistrature (Lévy), and which intensified some penalties but also "correctionalized" or demoted certain crimes to misdemeanors, because juries habitually had excused them whereas judges could be persuaded to convict (Passion, "La politique"; Ministère de la justice, *Compte-général de l'administration de la justice criminelle* [1880, published 1882], ix). This was to legalize a practice that the government had used unofficially at least since 1842, according to Schnapper, 205. Some Second Empire magistrates advocated even more radical reversals than this circumvention of the jury. Writing in 1868, Nouguier felt it necessary to refute colleagues who urged a return to inquisitorial, secret proceedings, and an end to extenuating circumstances: Nouguier, I: "Avant-propos," esp. xv. By 1867–68, reformists were accusing the government of unabashedly leading its judges. Prévost-Paradol launched a particularly outspoken attack on behalf of judicial independence, in the press and in his reform tract, *La nouvelle France*. While every new regime had purged the judiciary, the methods of the Second Empire were especially resented: in 1852, it imposed a retirement age which eliminated the older, less tractable magistrates and created the conditions for intense competition for posts and promotions throughout the system, dependent on favors to the administration (Prévost-Paradol, 156–171; Barrot, 76–84; Favre, 22–26; Georges Picot, *La Réforme judiciaire en France* [Paris: Hachette, 1881], 126–129). In 1859, it imposed new government controls over the assignment of particular judges to particular chambers, especially the notorious sixth chamber of the misdemeanors courts; while such controls had always applied to the Cour d'assises, the procedure became all the more obvious. In a book of 1860, the celebrated and politically independent lawyer Berryer protested the effects of government measures intended, he charged, to augment the authority of prosecutors and to force defense lawyers to adopt markedly subordinate language and behavior, staunching free speech in the courtroom as the government had done in the legislature and the press (in Moreau, "Introduction," ii-xx; also note the specific case cited by Moreau, 4). The independence of the magistrature was a key issue in the new legislatures of 1870 and 1871 (Picot, 133–139; Favre, 24–25). In the end, the government's own crime statistics were turned as evidence against this general policy. While a drop in the official statistics on

crime rates during the first thirteen years of the Empire had promoted the claim that firmer repression reduced crime and improved public mores, a new surge in offenses in the late 1860s cast doubt on that thesis (Wright, 95–98, 102; Lambert, 58–59; Ministère de la justice, *Compte-général de l'administration de la justice criminelle* [1868, pub. 1870], xxxiv-v).

142. See notes 47 and 48; Moses, chap. 7.

143. *Le Petit journal* (December 28, 1869): 1, elaborated the standard view: "L'or est partout, chatoyant aux yeux, souriant à l'imagination"—a decor that was contrasted to the severity of the affair and to the inadequacy of the room to accommodate its crowd. On the unseemliness of women: the *Gazette des tribunaux* (December 31, 1869), as cited in note 48.

144. This shift, associated with the Enlightenment and the ensuing implementation of Enlightenment values, is dramatized in Stephen Greenblatt's comment that from the early modern perspective construing masculinity as display, the modern male subject has been feminized: *Shakespearian Negotiations: The Circulation of Social Energy in Renaissance England* (Berkeley and Los Angeles: University of California Press, 1988), 87–88 and 183, note 36.

145. In the neoclassical courthouse, where normative law was emphasized over particular procedural practices, distinctions between civil and penal courtrooms were less significant for the decor of the courtroom. The standards of architectural practice are indicated by the model projects published by Gourlier (cited in note 79) and in the winning projects for courthouses periodically assigned for the annual Grand Prix de Rome competition, which were also published. On the latter, see the appendices of D. D. Egbert, *The Beaux-Arts Tradition in French Architecture* (Princeton: Princeton University Press, 1980); on the competition

for a courthouse for a Cour de cassation in 1824, see Neil Levine, "The Competition for the Grand Prix in 1824," in Robin Middleton, ed., *The Beaux-Arts and Nineteenth-Century French Architecture* (Cambridge, MA: MIT Press, 1982), 66–123, and especially the discussion of the winning project's text-celebrating iconography, developed through sculpture and culminating in inscriptions of the code above the bench, 105–107. Those standards also mark the plethora of extant courthouses themselves, which have not been systematically studied. Georges Teyssot, "La ville-équipement: la production architecturale des bâtiments civils, 1795–1848," *Architecture Mouvement Continuité* 45 (1978): 89, has estimated an average of 5.2 courthouses per year built in France during that period. On those of the Marne department in the region of Reims, see Daniel Imbault, *Un Siècle d'architecture publique: La Marne, 1830–1930* (Chalons-sur-Marne: Conseil d'architecture, d'urbanisme et d'environnement de la Marne, 1984), 51, who emphasizes the persistent conservatism of that architectural image of justice: "Même à la fin du XIXe siècle, le style néoclassique est le plus souvent utilisé dans la construction des palais de justice. Il semble que la fonction même de ces édifices oblige à n'utiliser que les ordres classiques, symbole de l'ordre esthétique et social, alors que dans la plupart d'autres constructions publiques, ceux-ci sont de plus en plus abandonnés permettant ainsi une spécificité formelle de chaque bâtiment affirmant la fonction de chacun." As Guadet pointed out at the end of the century, columns were inappropriate inside a criminal courtroom because they created hiding places in a room magistrates needed to survey: *Eléments et théorie*, 2: 489. (Ultimately that practical factor encouraging plain walls probably also encouraged a revival of richly carved ceilings, a rather anti-classical development, especially associated with the untrammelled early French Renais-

sance.) A powerful source of prescriptive influence favoring the replacement of illusionistic decoration and, indeed, paintings, by sculpture and inscriptions was Quatremère de Quincy, who had demonstrated his views in his well-known alteration of Soufflot's Panthéon in Paris.

146. On the location of the old courtroom relative to the reconstruction plan shown in fig. 14, see note 29. Jacques Wilhelm, "Une esquisse de Bon Boullongne [*sic*] pour le plafond de la IIe chambre des requêtes du Parlement de Paris," *Archives de l'art français* 22 (1959): 101–107; L. Guillmard, "La justice assure la paix et protège les arts. Une esquisse de Bon Boullogne pour le Palais de Justice," *Bulletin du Musée Carnavalet* 2 (1975): 1–12. The Paris administration commissioned Charles Maillot to remove the fresco from the room before its demolition. Although the original painting burned in situ in the Commune fire of 1871, Maillot produced a copy for the city museum, the Carnavalet. Département de la Seine, *Inventaire général des oeuvres d'art du Département de la Seine* (Paris: Chaix, 1883), 3: 66–67.

147. "La nouvelle cour d'assises à propos de la rentrée des tribunaux," *Le Petit journal* (November 3, 1868): 1–2: "Pour l'application des dernières sévérités de la loi, pour la condamnation à mort d'un coupable, il semblait au penseur que cette chambre était insuffisante. Elle nuisait, par son exiguïté, à la majesté de l'arrêt terrible. L'esprit public paraissait demander, pour l'exercise du plus étendu des droits de répression légale, un local monumental imposant, en harmonie avec les terribles fonctions de ceux qui y représentaient dignement la Défense de la Société et l'Obéissance aux Lois." For a later reminiscence of the old courtroom, which comes close to regretting its replacement, see Bérard, 1: 9–10: "Qui ne se souvient de cette vieille salle, étroite et sombre, . . . avec son plafond bas et des barreaux aux fenêtres

qui lui donnaient l'air d'une prison? . . . N'était-ce pas dans cette salle que Victor Hugo avait cherché ses inspirations, lorsqu'il dépeignait ainsi dans *Les Misérables* la Cour d'assises d'Arras . . . : 'L'obscurité, la laideur, la tristesse, et de tout cela se dégageait une impression austère et auguste, car on y sentait cette grande chose humaine qu'on appelle la loi et cette grande chose divine qu'on appelle la justice . . .'"

148. See note 48, for the assertion of male self-control of spontaneous emotional response shared with women, and on the phenomenon of the responsive courtroom public that censured itself after the fact. After Troppmann's trial, such self-criticism manifested itself even in the debates of the legislature: Drachline, chap. 14. Also see note 124, regarding the agitated reading of the verdict by the foreman; his agitation surely stemmed in part from the terrible consequences of his words, but also from the difficulty of situating his own interests in relation to the conflict of authority dramatized in the proceedings.

149. While the following account focuses on responses in the 19th-century press, the major 20th-century interpretations of the wing's west facade and vestibule (which exclude the courtroom) may be acknowledged here: Neil Levine has briefly analyzed Duc's west entrance as a theoretical response to Labrouste's Bibliothèque Sainte-Geneviève, in his dissertation and in his essay, "The Romantic Idea of Architectural Legibility: Henri Labrouste and the Néo-Grec," in Drexler, ed., *The Architecture of the Ecole des Beaux-Arts*, 348–349. On the issue of architecture and writing raised by Levine, see below. More recently David Van Zanten has devoted a chapter of his *Designing Paris: The Architecture of Duban, Labrouste, Duc, and Vaudoyer* (Cambridge, MA: MIT Press, 1987), to Duc's west entrance, treated as a signal event in the revival of classicism, which Van Zanten valuably relates to contem-

porary psychological aesthetics and Greek archeological theory, particularly the developing notion of architectural empathy, also important to my argument. What is not considered there is the larger socio-cultural context for the reinvestment of architecture with anthropomorphic content, and more specifically, the implications of the disturbingly fragmented character of Duc's architecture and its ability to provoke, yet frustrate, contemporary desire to interpret it.

150. Rigaud, 297: "[D]epuis huit jours on a pu juger de l'oeuvre des architectes. C'est même la première fois, je crois, que le public a été aussi franchement appelé à donner son avis. Est-ce que décidément on songerait à compter l'opinion public pour quelque chose?" The open house was announced in the press: "Faits divers," *Le Moniteur universel* (November 1, 1868): 1435; "Faits divers," *Le Temps* (October 28, 1868): 3; B. de Renjarde, "Chronique," *Le Petit journal* (October 31, 1868): 3, noted when and where to go.

151. The legislature's right to interpolate the cabinet was restored only in 1867, one of a series of gradual government concessions to parliamentary opposition. Normally Haussmann attempted to control the press response to his work through press releases: J. M. and B. Chapman, *The Life and Times of Baron Haussmann* (London: Weidenfeld & Nicolson, 1957), 151. In those cases, the existence of an official text is betrayed by similarities in commentaries in the press. When the Paris administration preceding Haussmann's formally unveiled Duc's restoration of a 16th-century clock face by Germain Pilon, allegorizing Force and Justice, in 1852, it provided such a text, a copy of which survives among Duc's papers. In the case of the new wing, however, reviews were diverse, and the patterns among them appear to arise from a discourse established through sequence of publication, rather than from any official line. It

144

is clear, however, that reviewers were given lists of artists who had contributed to the wing.

152. See the reports of construction progress presented to the Departmental Council by the Prefect of the Seine, especially those of October 10 and 21, 1875: Département de la Seine, *Procès-verbaux*.

153. The engraving of the facade in its "état actuel" accompanied a review by Grangedor, "Les derniers travaux d'art au Palais de Justice," *Gazette des beaux-arts* 25 (December 1, 1868): 509–531, fig. on 511. The more standard choice to show the facade as it would be completed is exemplified by the illustration for Rigaud's review of the new wing for *L'Illustration*, 246–247.

154. The canonical status of Vignola's 16th-century treatise on the orders while Duc was a student is attested by the architects Hippolyte Lebas and François Debret: "Il suffit de dire que, traduit de toutes les langues, publié sous tant de formes, souvent augmenté et jamais corrigé, les professeurs les plus habiles le regardent toujours comme l'ouvrage élémentaire propre à former les élèves qui se livrent à l'étude de l'architecture." Lebas and Debret, eds., *Oeuvres complètes de Jacques Barozzi de Vignole* (Paris: Didot, 1825), vol. 1, introduction.

For a late Second Empire discussion of the tradition of gender-typing in the orders, addressed to the general reader, see Charles Blanc, *Grammaire des arts du dessin* (Paris: Renouard, 1867), esp. 158–161. Blanc, 199, took issue with the ancient Roman treatise of Vitruvius for associating the richest of the orders with a maiden rather than a woman; it is interesting that Duc chastened what Blanc called his Corinthian capitals, giving them a still more youthful aspect.

155. These choices were exemplified by the buildings of two leading courts, the Palais of Paris with Desmaisons' Doric entrance facade at the east, and Baltard's Corinthian Palais de Justice for Lyon, and by the two most recent Grand Prix de Rome competition projects for courthouses, the Doric project for a Cour de cassation by Henri Labrouste of 1824 and the Corinthian project of F.-B. Boitte for a Cour de cassation of 1859. René de la Ferté, "Le monde des arts," *L'Artiste* (December 1, 1868): 411–412, called Duc's order Doric; the more common interpretation was Corinthian. On its combination of features: Charles Blanc, "Le nouveau Palais de Justice: I: Architecture," *Le Temps* (October 30, 1868): 3; François Lenormant, "Le nouveau Palais de Justice," *Moniteur des architectes* 3 (November 1, 1868): 163–171, esp. 166.

156. My interpretation of the capitals at the misdemeanors wing as force and justice is based on a contract drawing for the female-headed capital, dated 1852 and annotated by Duc, "deux têtes représentant la force et la justice," referring to its companion capital with a bearded face; the drawing is in the collection of the Service des bâtiments, Ville de Paris.

157. From left (north) to right (south), these are Prudence and Truth (both by the sculptor A. Dumont), Punishment and Protection (by Jouffroy), and Force and Justice (by Jaley).

158. Grangedor, esp. 512.

159. "Declaim" (*déclame*) is Duc's explicitly rhetorical term for what semioticians would call connotation; Duc's comments are quoted by Paul Sédille, "Joseph-Louis Duc, Architecte (1802–1879)," *Encyclopédie d'architecture*, 2nd series, 8 (1879): 70. Cambacérès' reports on drafts of the Code civil offer examples of the metaphor of juridical edifice: Fenet, ed., *Recueil complet des travaux préparatoires du Code civil*, 15 vols. (Paris, 1827–28), 1: 2 (1793), 99 (1794); also see Blanc's reference to this trope cited in note 177. Foucault's use of the term "legal edifice" exemplifies its persistence into the present: *Power/Knowledge*, 94.

160. If this order seemed to Blanc to gain robustness from its double role as ideal image and structural buttress, its ambiguous status ("mensongère") dissolved it to mere "simulacres de colonnes" for Grangedor, 513.

161. Sédille, 67–72, esp. 69; the drawings he cites, including figs. 43 & 44, survive in the collection of the Cour d'appel de Paris. Blanc, as will be clear below, also acknowledged Duc's indebtedness to early French Renaissance architecture, as well as the classical tradition of antiquity.

162. Sédille, 68, 70. Duc's letter as quoted by Sédille has become a frequent citation in architectural history of this period. I have commented on the implications that Duc and his colleagues attributed to arcuation and vaulting versus the post and lintel tradition in "Le Code et l'équité." See also Barry Bergdoll, *Les Vaudoyers. Une dynastie d'architectes*, exh. cat. (Paris: Réunion des musées nationaux, 1991), 53–59, esp. 56, a summary of Léon Vaudoyer's theory of architectural history, to be treated at greater length in Bergdoll, *The Reinvention of Time and Place: Léon Vaudoyer and the Politics of Historicism in French Architecture*, forthcoming from the Architectural History Foundation/MIT Press. The types of basilica and vaulted hall were articulated as such in graphic and built form during the mid-19th century. Beyond such established buildings as Hittorff's church of Saint Vincent de Paul, informed by that architect's studies of the ancient basilica (fig. 46) and inaugurated in 1844, the most recent basilican reconstruction in the public's memory would have been the Grand Prix laureate Julien Guadet's major project sent from Rome, a painstaking reconstruction of Trajan's forum featuring the Ulpian Basilica. It was exhibited in Paris in 1867, the year before the inauguration of the west wing of the Palais. See *Roma Antiqua. Forum, Colisée, Palatin*, exh. cat. (Paris: Académie de France à Rome, Ecole française de Rome, & the Ecole nationale supérieure des Beaux-Arts, 1985): 184–207. Although Guadet presented the basilica with an open-truss roof, the French Academy maintained that a flat ceiling was more likely (184). Duc himself justified his decision to give his west vestibule vaults in place of an earlier, less costly design for a flat ceiling, as a means to continue the French waiting hall tradition exemplified by the familiar 17th-century Salle des pas perdus at the Palais. See the prefect's report of December 18, 1862, presenting this revision: Département de la Seine, *Procès-verbaux*.

163. "Une volonté trop énergique," in the words of Grangedor, who disapproved of both Duc's compromised use of the order in the facade and his hyperactive vaults in the ceiling of the vestibule, where the classical tradition required repose, 516.

164. The parallel here, as Martha Ward has pointed out to me, stems from the assumption that Troppmann's maker has invested him with a psychology just as Duc has invested his architectural details with purpose. Duc's "conscientiousness" was a matter of near-universal comment; for instance, Grangedor's otherwise largely hostile review, 510, 518; Lenormant, 170; Constant Moyaux, manuscript draft of a review, c. 1872–1873, Getty Center, Los Angeles, record 22 (I am indebted to Robin Middleton for the latter). My dissertation (1167–1175) suggests that it was this aspect, a virtual thematization of the issue of artistic and visual conscience, that won Duc the emperor's handsome prize of 100,000 francs from a committee of artists representing a range of media. Nor is it accidental that Duc invested part of the prize to endow a novel competition at the French Academy to encourage the kind of work he felt his building represented: the study of expressive detailing. Duc's own surviving sketches for details of the wing (including fig. 50)

bear out the contemporary view that every flex and stretch of a molding was a matter of deliberate purpose—a purpose that was ascribed to the architecture as well as to its architect.

165. *L'Illustration* 52 (1868): 312; *Le Monde illustré* (December 5, 1868): 357.

166. Grangedor, 515. A rationale naturalizing such a change in coloration was offered by Charles Blanc in his *Grammaire*, 245: "[S]i le corps humain est à peu près monochrome au dehors, il contient à l'intérieur des colorations brillantes qu'annoncent déjà le vermillon de ses lèvres, et les tons variés de sa prunelle quand il ouvre ses paupières." The architect should emulate the model of the body: "la monochromie au dehors, la polychromie au dedans." A recent interpretation by the French magistrate Garapon assimilates this contrast to 20th-century archetypal symbolism which fosters an archetypal apolitical social order. Specifically, Garapon characterizes the common transition in French courthouses from masonry vestibules to courtrooms warmed by the color of wood panelling and upholstery and the heat of robed professionals and massed bodies as an arrival in a womb-like interior space, which symbolically helps to recreate a lost unity and security in a social body torn by crime (78). Similarly, Garapon views the transition from dark circulation areas to more brightly lit courtrooms as a symbolic enlightenment of the public, helping to enact the rebirth of social order (35–36).

167. This gradation was noted by the art critic Charles Clément, "Les nouvelles constructions au Palais de Justice," *Journal des débats* (November 17, 1868): 2.

168. Timothée Trimm [Léo Lespes], "La nouvelle Cour d'assises à propos de la rentrée des tribunaux," *Le Petit journal* (November 3, 1868): 1–2, noted that the former magistrate and minister of justice during the Restoration, Peyronnet, used to say in

passing Prud'hon's painting at the Louvre, "Voilà ce qu'il faudrait placer dans nos Tribunaux!" Trimm declared that Lehmann's paintings in the south courtroom fulfilled that wish; their iconography was similar to Bonnat's.

Prud'hon's painting was designed to hang above the judge's bench in the old criminal courtroom, in place of the crucifixion traditional to the ancien régime, and specifically in place of the word LOIS inscribed in gold on the wall at the time Prud'hon received the job. Commissioned as an image to replace text, but equally as a secular substitute for the crucifixion, it was intended to inspire a crime-deterring terror in the viewer. In 1815, during the pious Bourbon Restoration, it was retired in favor of a crucifixion at the instigation of the appellate court's President Séguier, who restored a number of ancien régime traditions at the Palais. In 1826, the Louvre acquired it from the city in exchange for four crucifixions to be hung in courtrooms. On its history and iconography, see especially Charles Clément, *Prud'hon, sa vie, ses oeuvres et sa correspondance* (Paris: Didier, 1872), 314–327, 333–337, 339, 341–343; Helen Weston, "Prud'hon: Justice and Vengeance," *Burlington Magazine* 117 (June 1975): 353–363; Sylvain Laveissière, *Prud'hon, La Justice et la Vengeance divine poursuivant le crime*, Les dossiers du Département des peintures 32 (Paris: Réunion des musées nationaux, 1986), esp. 14 (noting how Charles Blanc was the key figure to stimulate interest in the painting in the 1840s and again in the early 1860s—when Duc was considering how to decorate his courtrooms) and 104–106. An exhibition on Prud'hon in preparation in Paris promises to yield further commentary on this work.

169. Prud'hon also considered a scheme in which he treated vice as a couple, male and female, but rendered the virtuous victim female; he rejected this in favor of the male

criminal and victim. Yet commentators in the later 19th century remarked on the painting's gendered implications even so, noting the androgynous aspect of the male victim, described as ravishingly beautiful. The larger phenomenon of androgynous male nudes painted in the early 19th century has been explored by Abigail Solomon-Godeau as cited below in note 199.

170. Prosecutor Grandperret's image of revelatory light should be remembered here, although his version was Prud'hon's Vengeance with a torch—the avenging light that attaches itself to the criminal. Reciprocity between the decor of the courtroom and the figures used in trial speeches was at times literal. For instance, Bérard, 1: 208–09, recounted a famous *plaidoyer* made during the Restoration in the old criminal chamber when Prud'hon's painting still hung above the bench, in which the lawyer Moret pointed to the apprehensive criminal in Prud'hon's painting and declared that if such be the look of crime, his own client, serene and calm, could not be guilty. Daumier made several depictions of defense lawyers pointing to Prud'hon's painting or to a crucifixion above the judges: Weston, 362 and fig. 40; Jean Le Foyer, *Daumier au Palais de Justice* (Paris: La Colombe, 1958), plate 52.

171. Both the north and south courtrooms had crucifixions painted on gold grounds apparently in Byzantine, archaizing style: Blanc, "Le nouveau Palais de Justice: II: Peintures," *Le Temps* (November 18, 1868): 3; Clément. Clément described the crucifixion as the focus of light and attention in these courtrooms: "L'image du Christ, peinte sur or, encadrée d'une riche bordure sculptée, se détache sur le fond sobre qui l'entoure; c'est le point brillant de la décoration, qui attire et attache l'oeil dès l'entrée." Although the painters enjoyed a certain latitude in subject matter and style, subject to review by the city's Commission des beaux-

arts and by the architect, it is clearly not accidental that the two courtrooms, handled by different artists, both featured gold-ground crucifixions. It is probably significant that the early French Renaissance criminal courtroom at Rouen had a celebrated crucifixion with a gold ground—as well as a decor that served as a model for Duc. On the latter painting, see "Le Palais-de-Justice de Rouen," *Magasin pittoresque* 2 (1834): 110; it was restored in 1859: Victor Joliy, "Restauration de la relique du Palais de Justice de Rouen," *Revue des beaux-arts* 10 (1859): 115–117. The decor at the Palais in Paris also draws on the tradition of crucifixions in which Christ's halo literally radiates light, evoked even more specifically in the crucifixion of 1881 by Elie Delaunay for Duc's restored Grand'Chambre, and now in the Petit Palais of Paris.

172. Prime among the critics emphasizing the sensuousness of the room was Blanc, as quoted in the text below; Sorel, 1078; Faverie, 1036; Clément characterized the decoration overall as voluptuous and intimate; among the others, note especially Rigaud, 298: "La décoration est d'une richesse désolante. Le regard se noie dans l'or; il n'est pas jusqu'au Christ qui ne soit crucifié sur un fond d'or. C'est fâcheux. Une salle ou se rend la justice criminelle réclame plus de sévérité. Est-ce que la Justice, surtout celle qui a droit de vie et de mort, n'exige pas plus de simplicité, plus de gravité? Tant de richesse, tant d'apparat et de coquetterie nuit à sa grandeur et au respect qu'on lui doit, à la terreur qu'elle inspire." Blanc's reservations about the appropriateness of Bonnat's dramatic plasticity exemplify a widespread, though not universal, reaction.

173. The instability of the attribution of ethical character to the sexes had a particular political context in the late Empire, when the patriarchal emperor and Marianne, the allegorical mother of the Republic, competed for popular loyalty, and it again be-

came possible to call Louis-Napoléon the illegal upstart and Marianne the patriot.

174. The facade and vestibule refer iconographically to Napoléon I, with eagles and portrait medallions on the exterior, and a sequence of four legislator-kings culminating in Napoléon I, who overlook the vestibule from niches in its end walls.

175. Lawyers would invoke this painting to remind magistrates of the unjust suffering of Christ at the hands of his judges; for an example from the Dreyfus trial, see Damien, 469. Like many crucifixions made for the Palais, Bonnat's painting drew on the celebrated model that had hung in the original and, after 1830, in a copy, in the old criminal courtroom (fig. 57): the 17th-century crucifixion by Philippe de Champaigne, installed at the Louvre in 1871. On the latter, see Bernard Dorival, *Philippe de Champaigne, 1602–1674: La vie, l'oeuvre et le catalogue raisonné de l'oeuvre*, 2 vols. (Paris: Laget, 1976), 1: 51, 77–79, 142; 2: # 67, 44–45. Dorival notes Champaigne's importance in purging the crucifixion of accessory figures (including, one might note, the flanking thieves), as well as his seeming compliance with the Council of Trent's injunction to avoid emphasizing the corporeal suffering of Christ. The latter is explicitly what interested Bonnat when he received the commission in 1872, as critics recognized at its presentation in the Salon of 1874. On Bonnat's procedure and on the criticism, see Achille Fouquier, *Léon Bonnat, première partie de sa vie et de ses ouvrages* (Paris: Imprimerie D. Jouaust, 1879), 215–219, who paraphrases the word of the critics thus: "M. Bonnat n'a pas peint un Christ en croix, mais le mauvais larron" (216–217). Similarly Louis Gonse wrote in his "Salon de 1874. I," *Gazette des beaux-arts* (June 1, 1874): 510–511: "[C]ette figure ne sera point déplacée à la cour d'assises et . . . les habitués du lieu y reconnaîtront avec plaisir l'un des leurs." The painting and the obligatory *esquisse* submitted for it are now at the Petit Palais, Paris, having been removed from the Palais with all other crucifixions at the time of the separation of church and state in 1904. Richomme was in fact commissioned to repaint his crucifixion in 1871, but the administration apparently thought better of replacing it in the criminal courts, and it was ultimately hung in another courtroom in the appellate courts. The commission dates for Richomme's replacement and Bonnat's crucifixion are given in the Archives de la Ville de Paris, 10624/72/1, liasse 10, Bonnat folder, and liasse 163, Richomme folder. My thanks to Alisa Luxenberg for sharing her knowledge of Bonnat with me.

176. A copy of the print is among the drawings in the architects' archives, now in the collection of the Cour d'appel de Paris. In 1863, Duc had prepared a project for redoing the Grand'Chambre, still in its bare state, which entailed an enriched version of the decor he had used in other civil courtrooms, but not a historical reconstruction. Continually postponed, it was still unexecuted in 1871 when the Commune fires destroyed the room completely. In the planning for its reconstruction, beginning in 1871, it was notably Duc and his assistant Daumet who pleaded for a historical reconstruction of the early 16th-century decor, particularly the ceiling (Archives de la ville de Paris, D5N4/1); after prolonged debate, the historical project was approved and the courtroom inaugurated in 1879. It would have been possible to restore it with its medieval vaults, and it is significant that this was not done, perhaps because no one then upheld the medieval vaulted chamber as an appropriate type for a courtroom—partly for acoustic reasons. For an indication of the exoticism of the early 16th-century French courtroom, with its sheer walls and heavily sculpted ceiling, to mid-19th-century commentators used to a more architectonic

decor clearly supporting a reposeful ceiling, see Stabenrath, *Le Palais de Justice de Rouen* (Rouen, 1842), 97, who describes "la sévérité de ses murailles nues. . . . la pesanteur de son admirable plafond noir et doré, orné d'arabesques, et qui semble prêt à tomber sur le spectateur comme le châtiment sur le coupable . . ." (While the *Magasin pittoresque* published brief articles on the Grand' Chambre of Paris and the courtroom at Rouen in 1834 with admiring commentary, its point of view was atypical and was probably marked by architects who were friends of Duc's and deeply interested in the French Renaissance: Léon Vaudoyer and Albert Lenoir.) Guadet's treatise testifies to the institutionalization of the French courtroom formulated in the late Middle Ages and early Renaissance as a type for modern practice by the end of the 19th century, 2: 487–488.

177. "Le nouveau Palais de Justice: I": "Quel caractère doit avoir de nos jours un palais de justice? Doit-il être sévère, terrible? On le penserait tout d'abord, d'après l'idée qu'on se forme de la justice, toujours confondue dans notre esprit avec l'idée de châtiment, et toujours assombrie par l'image éloignée, mais persistante, du bourreau. Toutefois, quand on y réfléchit, on conçoit qu'une expression de férocité ne conviendrait plus à la justice présente, et encore moins à la justice future. Avant la Révolution, les parlements étaient d'une cruauté horrible. En dépit des protestations de Montaigne et de la philosophie, ils appliquaient quelquefois, même en matière civile, la question des coins, la torture des brodequins, celle du plomb fondu dans les oreilles et autres inventions imitées des brigands. J'ai lu dans le *Journal de Barbier*, si j'ai bonne mémoire, qu'un jeune garçon ayant volé à un médecin sa montre dans la salle même ou l'on rendais la justice, fut jugé séance tenante, condamné à être pendu, et exécuté sur l'heure! Pour élever un monument où des magistrats rendraient encore de pareils arrêts, aucune architecture, ce me semble, ne serait assez farouche. C'est à peine si un temple de Paestum y suffirait, avec ses supports trapus, son architrave formidables, ses rudes triglyphes, et l'âpreté de ses entre-colonnements et la violence de ses profils. Eh bien! qui le croirait? ces parlements étaient somptueusement logés. Ils voulaient que l'enceinte de la justice rivalisât de magnificence avec les demeures de la royauté. Je ne parle pas même de l'ancien Palais de Justice de Paris, qui avait été longtemps habité par les rois, et où Saint Louis fit élever cette chapelle, si artistement, si savemment restaurée par M. Viollet-le-Duc; mais les autres parlements du royauté, celui de Rouen, par exemple, et celui de Rennes étaient splendides. Le palais du parlement de Normandie était un merveille d'architecture. Celui du parlement de Rennes étalaient des splendeurs rares, avait des lambris du plus beau travail, des soffites à caissons sculptés et dorés, dont les fonds étaient peints par Jouvenet. Les magistrats y étaient logés et meublés comme les princes de la justice. C'est en se rattachant à ces traditions que M. Duc a déterminé le caractère qu'il donnerait au nouveau palais de la loi. Il s'est dit que dans la civilisation moderne, la justice devait se présenter à l'esprit, non pas tant comme une menace que comme une protection; que ce palais bâti pour l'avenir devait témoigner des sentiments plus humains auxquels nous ont amenés les progrès de la philosophie et l'adoucissement des moeurs; que si l'on s'étaient permis tant de pompe dans les anciens prétoires, à plus forte raison pouvait-on se permettre aujourd'hui de tempérer par quelque élégance la majesté voulue dans "l'édifice de nos lois," comme disent les gens de robe. M. Duc est parti de cette idée. . . . [In the courtrooms themselves:] Ici reparaissent l'ampleur, le confort et la magnificence que l'architecte a cru devoir se permet-

tre en mémoire des anciens parlements, et suivant l'idée qu'il s'est formée de la justice moderne."

178. See Duc's text for a prize that he established, cited in note 192.

179. Bérard, 1: 255: "Aujourd'hui, les lits de justice sont tenus par l'opinion."

180. "Le nouveau Palais de Justice: I": "J'avoue que, pour mon compte, j'ai de la peine à me représenter une cour d'assises pompeusement décorée. Je me figure un malheureux homme, conseillé par la misère, après avoir été abruti par l'ignorance, qui est amené là en blouse pour rendre compte d'un vol ou d'un crime, sous ces plafonds dorés, vermillonnés et illustrés par de superbes peintures. Que pensera ce pauvre homme d'une société qui a dépensé tant d'argent pour le condamner et si peu d'argent pour l'instruire? Mais c'est affaire aux publicistes et aux philosophes de reprocher, s'il y a lieu, à l'architecte du Palais de Justice le luxe qu'il a déployé dans l'enceinte où se découvrent les plaies de l'humanité. Pour nous, n'ayant à envisager que la question d'art, nous ne marchanderont pas les éloges à un artiste qui a renouvelé avec tant de savoir et tant de goût, les traditions de magnificence auxquelles il entendait se rattacher."

181. "Monument de juillet élevé sur la place de la Bastille," *Revue générale de l'architecture* 1 (1840): 750–751, 757.

182. Foucault, "Tales of Murder," in *I, Pierre Rivière*, esp. 205–208. This was a familiar worry for presidents of criminal courts: Lambert, for example, enjoined his readers not to forget society as they absorbed themselves in the defendant's life, e.g., 104–105, 164.

183. Narjoux, *Paris*, 1: 37–38: "Les salles d'audiences sont très riches, trop riches même, a-t-on dit, sans bien se rendre compte de l'impression que de telles salles sont destinées à produire non seulement sur l'esprit des accusés qui y sont amenés, mais encore sur l'esprit des jurés qui doivent les juger. L'influence du milieu dans lequel tout homme se trouve placé est indiscutable, et c'est surtout lorsqu'il est assis sur le siège des coupables, ou lorsqu'il se trouve érigé en juge, que cette influence doit s'exercer et l'émouvoir. Dans une salle quelconque, froide, mesquine, le juré ne recevra aucune impression propre à lui faire comprendre la gravité du rôle qui lui incombe, le poids de la terrible responsabilité qu'il assume. Dans un local dont, au contraire, les formes, les proportions, la décoration sont une chose inaccoutumée, pouvant l'étonner et le surprendre, ses émotions sont tout autres, il se sent hors de son milieu, dans une situation exceptionnelle et anormale. Quant à l'accusé, quelque endurci qu'il soit, peut-il se défendre d'être involontairement, sinon ému, du moins impressionné par l'appareil qui l'entoure, l'éclat qui le frappe et l'étonne? Il se trouve tout à coup transporté de sa sombre cellule dans un milieu plein de splendeur; les peintures, les dorures miroitent devant ses yeux; il sent tous les regards fixés sur lui; il voit, un à un, lentement apparaître en faisant bruire leurs longues robes, les magistrats qui vont décider de son sort; il les voit prendre place sur un siège élevé, presque un trône, d'où ils dominent la foule respectueuse et empressée; il peut alors comparer son misérable état à la situation qu'il aurait pu acquérir ou conserver, et souvent, peut-être, s'élève dans son coeur comme une vague aspiration qui le ramènera au bien. Pour une telle mise en scène, qui ne peut être exempte de quelque apparence théâtrale, il ne faut pas un cadre ordinaire, il faut l'emploi de moyens violent, et l'un de ces moyens a consisté dans la création de salles splendides, richement décorées, augmentant le prestige de cette organisation sociale au nom de laquelle va être frappé celui qu'elle traduit devant elle." Concerning the involvement of the city in

this publication, see the Archives de la ville de Paris, VR1, minutes of November 20 & 28, 1876.

Before Narjoux, Lenormant also attributed the richness of the room to the administration and the courts. In paraphrasing and modifying Blanc's review for the architectural press in 1868, he pointedly rephrased Blanc's comment, "[N]'ayant à envisager que la question d'art, nous ne marchanderont pas les éloges à un artiste qui a renouvelé . . . les traditions de magnificence auxquelles il entendait se rattacher" as "Nous aurions à faire de sérieuses réserves sur le programme qui avait été ici donné à M. Duc. . . . [I]ci nos critiques portent sur le programme fourni à l'artiste, non sur la manière dont il l'a rempli . . ." (169).

184. Mona Ozouf, *Festivals and the French Revolution* (Paris: Gallimard, 1976; Eng. trans. Alan Sheridan, Cambridge, MA: Harvard University Press, 1988), passim, esp. chap. 8. It should be noted, however, that Ozouf here defines theater as the contemplative, passive spectacle such as Diderot and others sought to bring about, rather than the more disputative traditions invoked in the mid- to late 19th-century characterization of the criminal courts.

185. This tension between the hope that impressive ritual could reinforce the values of social order, the need for such rituals to seem spontaneous in order to be persuasive, and the problem that spontaneity might reveal divergences of values is evident in the interpretation of the social function of the criminal trial given by the contemporary magistrate Antoine Garapon, 138–156, and 157–159.

186. Bérard, I: 16–17: "Lorsqu'elle sortit des mains des ouvriers, . . . la salle était ruisselante d'or, la dorure dominait les tons sombres, et tout étincelait; l'architecte qui montrait pour la première fois la salle au premier président de la Cour, M. Devienne, attendait avec impatience ses impressions;

mais celui-ci lui dit froidement, de la façon distinguée dont M. Devienne disait finement des choses profondes: 'Avec une salle pareille, il faudra mettre aux accusés des habits de soie.'"

187. On the demand of the national Conseil des bâtiments civils for greater severity, see the Archives nationales, F21* 2542/17, minutes of July 25, 1853. For Delangle, see the publication of engravings and documents (including a report by Delangle) that he helped prepare: Département de la Seine, *Documents relatifs aux travaux du Palais de Justice*, esp. 226–227. An incomplete run of minutes of the departmental Commission des beaux-arts, mainly 1861–1866, a rare instance of departmental documents that survived the Commune fire of 1871 at the Hôtel de Ville, is available at the Archives de la ville de Paris, VR1. The administrative process by which the criminal courts project was developed is discussed in my dissertation.

188. Jacques Derrida (on the matter of whose shoes Van Gogh painted), "Restitutions of Truth to Size, *De la vérité en pointure*," *Research in Phenomenology* 8 (1978), 1–44.

189. Those same conditions that led Marx to publish his account of the commodity fetish in 1867, and were the basis of Benjamin's suggestive reading of material culture of the period in his Paris Arcades project, partially published as *Charles Baudelaire*. My understanding of the term fetish is guided by William Pietz's broad historical and cultural interpretation: "The Problem of the Fetish, I and II," *Res* 9 (Spring 1985): 5–17, and *Res* 13 (Spring 1987): 23–45. Pietz emphasizes aspects of the fetish which are relevant here, such as: its conjunction of desire and material object; the lack of transcendence of material object by thought; the object's persuasive unification of evidently heterogeneous, fragmentary elements, yet its appearance of disrupted or inverted social

value; the generative importance of social and cultural confrontation for its production.

190. Neil Levine, "The Book and the Building: Hugo's Theory of Architecture and Labrouste's Bibliothèque Ste-Geneviève," in Middleton, ed., *The Beaux-Arts*, 138–173; on Duc's facade and vestibule, "The Romantic Idea," in Drexler, ed., 348–49, and "Architectural Reasoning in the Age of Positivism: the Néo-Grec Idea of Henri Labrouste's Bibliothèque Sainte-Geneviève," Ph.D. diss., Yale University, 1975, 119–127; for the quotation from Levine, on legible architecture, "The Romantic Idea," 408.

191. This difference may bear relation to Pietz's distinction between the "metaphoric logic" of idols in the European Christian tradition and the "metonymic logic" of the fetish in the life of colonial Europe: *Res* 13 (1987): 45.

192. Not only the letter by Duc to a colleague, published by Sédille (cited in note 162), but also Duc's statement of the purpose of the prize he established to encourage the study of architectural detailing: Institut de France, *Mélanges 1871* (Paris, 1871), "Académie des Beaux-Arts, séance publique annuelle; programme des prix proposés," 5–7; reprinted by Daly in "Les hautes études en architecture: Le Prix Duc," *Revue générale de l'architecture* 29 (1872): 33–34.

193. The standard definition of publicity in juridical literature refers to a live audience; for a late 19th-century definition of "public" as the readership of publications, as opposed to an assembled crowd, see Tarde.

194. Cruppi, 86: "L'impression que produira sur eux telle ou telle déclaration resultera presque toujours de l'apparence extérieure, de la *plastique* du témoignage" [Cruppi's emphasis].

195. Foucault discussed the masking of disciplinary surveillance deploying non-representational power by spectacle based on the premise, indeed representation, of sovereign right, in *Discipline and Punish*, esp. 216–217, 221–223; "Two Lectures," in *Power/Knowledge*, 78–108. But it must also be stressed that Foucault was concerned with an interrelationship between sovereignty and the disciplinary, as in "The Eye of Power," *Power/Knowledge*, esp. 152, where he particularly linked the Rousseauian transposition of sovereignty from the king to the individual with the French reception of Bentham's normalizing panoramically available panopticon.

196. Foucault, "On the Genealogy of Ethics," in Paul Rabinow, ed., *The Foucault Reader* (New York: Pantheon, 1984), 343, quoted by Martin Jay, "In the Empire of the Gaze: Foucault and the Denigration of Vision in Twentieth-Century French Thought," in David Couzens Hoy, ed., *Foucault: A Critical Reader* (Oxford: Basil Blackwell, 1986), 195: "My point is not that everything is bad, but that everything is dangerous."

197. On the king's head: Foucault, *The History of Sexuality, Volume 1: An Introduction*, trans. Robert Hurley, orig. pub. Paris, 1976 (New York: Vintage Books, 1990), 88–89. For summary comment on the implications of change in political economy: Foucault, "Lecture Two," *Power/Knowledge*, 104–105. Jay's article, which characterizes Foucault's emphasis on transparency as "anti-ocular," is cited in the preceding note. The opposite interpretation is given by John Rajchman, "Foucault's Art of Seeing," *October* 44 (Spring 1988): 88–117, who describes Foucault's attempt to make visible the piercing gaze as a visual strategy that is redemptive, and who endorses Foucault's argument that material objects obstruct that effort. My concern here is primarily to clarify that two modes of visibility are at issue. For an instance of growing critical interest in the subject and in the material object that

looks back—as they seemed to do in the Paris courthouse—see Michael Ann Holly, "Past Looking," *Critical Inquiry* 16 (Winter 1990): 371–396.

198. See Rajchman's extension of Foucault's metaphor of visible mask vs. immaterial panoptic space into "the neo-Classical facades of panoptic prison architecture," emphasizing the separation and lack of relationship between the two, and the need to attend to space rather than material facade (Rajchman, 105). Foucault was less explicit about the architectural realm, and at times backed off from his own depth metaphors, as when he noted that discipline should not be construed simply as the invisible reality that underlies and gives the lie to visible sovereignty: "Lecture Two," in *Power/ Knowledge*, 106: "This is not to suggest that there is on the one hand an explicit and scholarly system of right which is that of sovereignty, and on the other hand, obscure and unspoken disciplines which carry out their shadowy operations in the depths, and thus constitute the bedrock of the great mechanism of power. In reality, the disciplines have their own discourse."

199. On painting: T. J. Clark, *The Painting of Modern Life: Paris in the Art of Manet and his Followers* (Princeton: Princeton University Press, 1984), who takes up Guy Debord's issue of spectacle for the Second Empire; Michael Fried, "Manet's Modernism," Bradley Foundation Lectures delivered at the University of Chicago, April 8, 10, 11, 1991, forthcoming from the University of Chicago Press. A history of 19th-century French viewers and viewing is in progress; for example, Jonathan Crary, *Techniques of the Observer: On Vision and Modernity in the Nineteenth Century* (Cambridge, MA: MIT Press, 1990), which poses the question in Foucauldian terms, and lectures presented at the 1992 meeting of the College Art Association: Abigail Solomon-Godeau's "Male Trouble: A Crisis in Representation," and Jann Matlock's "Exhibiting and Exposing: Historicizing the Gaze."

INDEX